AURORA BOREALIS
Mittens

Aurora Borealis Mittens

ISBN 13 (print): 978-1-937513-52-8

ISBN 13 (e-book): 978-1-937513-53-5

First Edition
Published by Cooperative Press
http://www.cooperativepress.com

Patterns © 2015, Shannon Okey except Nordic Stars Tam by Kim Benefiel Craigs
Text © 2015 Shannon Okey except thrumming tutorial and Latvian braid directions by Christina Bowers
Photos © 2015, Caro Sheridan
Models: Claire Turner, Holly Benna, Heather Benna

Cover image of northern lights by Artz Win Studio, licensed through Creative Market: http://crtv.mk/syJd
Sheep photo in Fannar pattern © Daniel Paul Moore, licensed through Creative Market: http://crtv.mk/tyHj
Aurora Borealis photo in Thora pattern © Artz Win Studio, licensed through Creative Market: http://crtv.mk/cyLc

Every effort has been made to ensure that all the information in this book is accurate at the time of publication; however, Cooperative Press neither endorses nor guarantees the content of external links referenced in this book.

If you have questions or comments about this book, or need information about licensing, custom editions, special sales, or academic/corporate purchases, please contact Cooperative Press: info@cooperativepress.com or 13000 Athens Ave C288, Lakewood, OH 44107 USA

No part of this book may be reproduced in any form, except brief excerpts for the purpose of review, without prior written permission of the publisher. Thank you for respecting our copyright.

Guess what? There's a bonus tam pattern, too.

For Cooperative Press

Senior Editor: Shannon Okey
Art Director: Elizabeth Green Musselman
Technical Editor: Andi Smith

AURORA BOREALIS
Mittens

Shannon Okey

knitgrrl.com

Contents

Nordic Inspiration | 6
Techniques and how-to | 8
Epic knitters: the saga | 104
Heroic dyers | 105
Sources for the curious | 106

Solveig page 16

Sigrun page 20

Fannar page 24

Thora page 26

Nordic Star page 32

Aud page 38

Halldora page 44

Aslaug page 50

Eydis page 56

Astrid page 62

Idunn's Garden page 68

Freydis page 76

Sindri page 82

Dagmar page 88

Gulla page 94

Nordic Stars Tam page 100

MATCH YOUR MITTENS TO YOUR BIKE
DOUBLE KNIT THEM IF YOU LIKE
RIB THE CUFFS AND WARM YOUR WRISTIES
BRIGHTEN COLD DAYS WITH THESE MITTSIES

Nordic Inspiration

Why knit mittens? Do you even need to ask?

If you aren't normally a mitten or glove knitter, there's much to recommend them. They're like a human body in miniature, offering copious opportunities for shaping and exquisite detail, enough to keep any knitter interested. But for me, it's all about color and pattern opportunities…

The patterns in this book have a lot in common, starting with the *Íslensk sjónabók* (*Ornaments and Patterns found In Iceland*). This book, a collaboration between the Iceland Academy of the Arts, The National Museum and The Home Industry Association, contains more than 700 pages filled with patterns from textiles and other items found in Icelandic museums.

Íslensk sjónabók is an enormous brain-buffet for creative knitters like us. Not only are there the expected motifs such as stars (typical even today in Norwegian sweaters and the like), but also animal figures, florals, architectural ornaments and so much more. Drawn from knitted, embroidered, and woven pieces, this book puts an enormous, concentrated amount of creative inspiration in one single place, and it got my design-mojo working!

I wanted to offer you more than just a motif slapped on a mitten. To manipulate existing patterns into something new. If the pattern looked like an ornamental iron gate, I cut and pasted design sections together to make it appear even more so. A palm pattern resembling seed pods got paired with florals on the main section of the hand, an almost Islamic-tile-like pattern was shifted to resemble tiles in Tangiers or Samarkand more closely than something emerging from the north, and so forth.

Then there's color. Millions of us are rabid fans of hand-dyed yarn, and these patterns are designed with that in mind. But they can be made just as beautiful with widely available solid colored yarns. Given the exact same skein of yarn, dyes and equipment, two talented hand dyers will somehow manage to make their work distinct from each other. It makes what we knit that much more special. (Many patterns in this book are knit, or have a second sample knit, in Knit Picks Palette).

Each pattern is knit in just two colors. Many mittens have been knit both ways, i.e. one mitten is knit with Color 1 as its motif color and Color 2 as the background, while the other is knit with Color 1 as background and Color 2 as motif. It's a fast way to show you how very different the mittens will look if you choose to work them in one way or the other. You, of course, can pick your favorite and knit both mittens the same if you like.

Some of these yarns come in big skeins that would allow you to knit more than one pair of mittens; perhaps you might want to buy the bigger skeins and divide them with someone from your knitting group? Alternately, we've given you a bonus hat pattern on page 100 designed to use up some of your leftovers.

I've tried to incorporate even more flexibility into each pattern by giving you your choice of bottom cuffs through one of my favorite techniques, provisional cast on. Many of these mittens are longer than the average pattern available today, which is something I personally happen to like (*no exposed skin between your inner sleeve and coat sleeve when it's negative who-knows-what outside!*). Sometimes, though, it's good to have a choice, and even if you decide to leave off additional cuff work on the mitten, I believe that bind offs looks much better worked from the opposite direction. It's just one of many small details that will help you customize these patterns to your own taste.

Techniques and how-to

THERE ARE A LOT OF SMALL THINGS THAT ADD UP IN A mitten pattern, from the cast-on used, to the liner (if you opt for a double thick and cushy hand covering), to yarns chosen, thumb shapings, cuff treatments, blocking, and finishing. In this section, we'll show you how to make your mittens as beautiful as they can be!

Needle and Gauge

All of the mittens in this book are designed to be knit at a gauge of 8 stitches to the inch. For some of the more complex patterns, this makes sizing up and down much easier, and if you are an exceptionally loose or tight knitter, you'll be able to go up or down in needle size to achieve gauge rather than driving yourself crazy with our recommended needle sizes. Always remember, not just for the purposes of this book, that the recommended needle size is a suggestion, not an absolute. Knitters knit differently and that's ok!

You should also know that many knitters achieve varying gauges with needles made of different materials. It's not you, boo—it's the bamboo! If you can't get gauge, try switching to metal needles from wood, or vice versa.

Some knitters may even find a difference in their gauge based on needle tip types (sharper lace needles work better for some knitters when working with finer weight yarns, it's all a matter of preference).

If you're an experienced knitter, none of this should be news to you—we've all had That Project where our gauge varied wildly because we were under stress, or sick, or even just distracted. Don't let this put you off if you're a newer knitter, though! I don't mean to scare you, I just want you to be armed with the best possible information so that you know you aren't a "bad" knitter if you can't get gauge, you simply may need to make some minor adjustments.

When it comes to swatching for a project like this, you really should be using not only the needles you intend to use throughout, but also the stitch configuration you intend.

Mittens are knit in the round, which means you can use four or five double-pointed needles, two short circulars or even magic loop to knit the patterns. *So why are you knitting your gauge swatches flat?* Knit your swatch in the round using the same needles and setup you intend to knit for the real thing: minor gauge

	ROUND GAUGE		
	8 STS/INCH	7 STS/INCH	6 STS/INCH
54 STS	6.75 IN/17.14 CM, UNBLOCKED	7.71 IN/19.58 CM, UNBLOCKED	9 IN/22.86 CM, UNBLOCKED
66 STS	8.25 IN/20.95 CM, UNBLOCKED	9.42 IN/23.92 CM, UNBLOCKED	11 IN/27.94 CM, UNBLOCKED
74 STS	9.25 IN/23.5 CM, UNBLOCKED	10.57 IN/26.85 CM, UNBLOCKED	12.33 IN/31.32 CM, UNBLOCKED

differences are very much amplified in a small project like a mitten. There's far less wiggle room when a something is small but has a lot of stitches. See examples of how quickly (and significantly!) a pattern can change size if gauge is off in the chart on the previous page.

When you take the time to work a gauge swatch, it will pay off (I promise)! My favorite way to do this is to cast on provisionally, and work a couple inches of the chart pattern. If all is well with your gauge, then you can pick up your cuff stitches at the end of your knitting and work the cuff of your choice, ending with a nice, stretchy bind off. This is particularly nice if you want a good, tight ribbing because the sudden transition between ribbing and colorwork pattern stitches in a small project like this can give you a false sense (of confidence or of doom!) when it comes to gauge.

And yes, I know swatching feels like a waste of time sometimes, but at least if you do it provisionally, you won't even have to pull out any stitches if you're perfectly on gauge. It's also simpler to switch to a new needle size to adjust your own personal tension once the project is cast on and actively being worked. As you can see in the chart on the prior page, just one or two stitches off gauge can make a huge difference in the width of your mitten. Similar results can be seen for height.

Casting On

As mentioned above, the most flexible cast on, in my opinion, is the long tail provisional cast on. I recommend this cast on for a variety of reasons in many of my patterns. Whether you're knitting a top-down raglan sweater or a mitten cuff, no one wants a tight, inflexible opening in their knitwear. This cast on will help you avoid it, and give you maximum flexibility for finishing the piece. It also wastes less yarn when you're determining how much you need to cast on, which helps you preserve special or expensive yarns.

Long tail provisional cast on is very simple: instead of regular long tail using one strand of yarn, slipknotted a few yards in, you'll use your working yarn and a piece of waste yarn to cast on. I recommend cotton dishcloth yarn if you have it, it doesn't rub fibers off onto your working yarn, it's sturdy, and it's cheap. Keep a ball on hand in your must-have knitting supplies!

After you've cast on all the stitches to your needle, drop off the first slipknot (it doesn't count as a stitch). Join the round, being careful not to twist. Knit 3 rounds until your stitches are even and then place a marker at the beginning of the round to mark the start of your first chart (back of hand). Place another marker at the start of your palm chart. Continue knitting.

The waste yarn will stay in place while you're knitting the remainder of the pattern. When it's time to work your cuffs, you'll remove the waste yarn and place live stitches back on the needle.

Working with Charts

Everyone is different when it comes to working charts, but the charts in this book are a bit on the complex side, so here are a few tips for successful completion.

Mark your place

This isn't just when you put your pattern down for the night! Some of the patterns are not very repetitive, so it's easy to lose your place. There are many different tools available, including pattern markers and highlighter tape. Or, you can simply mark off your pattern lines on a photocopy of the chart as you go along. Some people love magnetic chart holders, too!

I'm very partial to Knit Companion, a software tool available at knitcompanion.com and on the Apple App Store. Knit Companion allows you to mark up your patterns from inside the app itself, as well as keep track of color changes, stitches and so much more.

Prep your yarn

Some of the patterns in this book use gradient yarn kits to produce color effects, such as Idunn's Garden. Each color in the progression comes as a single skein, though. Take the time to divide each yarn color in the progression into two equal skeins. If you really want to make things easy on yourself, use the Russian join or spit-splicing technique to then connect the individual colors to each other in the appropriate sequence. This comes in handy if you tend to take your knitting with you (less chance of losing a tiny skein of something!).

Even if you're only using two colors, it's nice to have two equal skeins to start for each mitten, and makes for a smaller project bag to carry along, particularly with some of the larger yarn skeins shown here. Or, as previously recommended, perhaps you might be splitting a larger skein of hand-dyed yarn with a friend?

An easy way to make equal skeins is to weigh the skein at the beginning, start balling, then weigh the ball as you go along until it weighs half of the original amount. Snip and continue balling the second half. Use a kitchen or postal scale. (For those of you in the US, many post offices have scales available in their automated mailing stations! No need to endure funny looks from the counter staff).

Advanced sharing

Opting to split an extra-large skein with a friend? If you know how many yards or meters of yarn you need (approximately), you can determine how many ounces or grams of yarn to take from the big skein like this:

Using information from your chosen yarn's label, divide the length by the weight. Using Cephalopod Yarns' Skinny Bugga as an example (used in Sindri, page 82):

4 oz = 424 yards

114 gm = 388 meters

Every ounce of yarn is, therefore, approximately 106 yards (or expressed in metric terms, 38 gm is about 130 meters). Weigh as you go along and you'll know how many yards you have in each ball to divide equally without having to re-wind multiple times.

Finishing

If you've used the recommended provisional long tail cast on, once you've finished knitting, you'll need to remove the waste yarn and either bind off as is or move on to a new cuff treatment with your live stitches back on the needles.

Cuff treatments

Here are a few of our favorite mitten cuffs. Don't be shy! If you have a favorite pattern you'd like to try instead of the recommended pattern or patterns shown, do it!

It's easy to rip back to the first round of extra stitches you left on the needle if you want to start over and try a different one. You may find that the mitten is too big on your wrist, for example, so a 1x1 ribbing is more appropriate than corrugated rib or 2x2.

Cuff Option 1

I-cord cast on: with DPNs in the appropriate size, cast on 4 stitches. Do not turn.

Step 1: Slide your stitches back to the beginning of the needle.

Step 2: K3, kfb to attach cord to mitten bottom.

Step 3: Slip all stitches back to LH needle.

Repeat steps 2 and 3 until you have the required number of stitches plus 3.

Bind off the first three stitches and weave in any ends.

Cuff Option 2

Latvian braid (above, on Aslaug) is one technique that I just find easier to understand via video.

Sometimes it just helps to see the stitches being worked. WEBS has an excellent one online at

http://www.yarn.com/videos/video/how-to-knit-a-latvian-braid/

Or see page 14 for even more about this technique and Latvia's Viking connection.

Cuff Option 3

1 x 1 rib (multiple of 2 sts)

Cast on required number of stitches.

Rnd 1: [K1, p1], repeat to end of rnd.

Repeat rnd 1.

Cuff Option 4

2 x 2 rib (multiple of 4 sts)

Cast on required number of stitches.

Rnd 1: [K2, p2], repeat to end of rnd.

Repeat rnd 1.

Cuff Option 5

1 x 1 corrugated rib (multiple of 2 sts)

Cast on required number of sts in MC.

Rnd 1: [With CC, p1, with MC, k1], repeat to end of rnd.

Repeat rnd 1.

Cuff Option 6

2 x 2 corrugated rib (multiple of 4 sts)

Cast on required number of sts in MC.

Rnd 1: [With CC, p2, with MC, k2], repeat to end of rnd.

Repeat rnd 1.

Cuff Option 7

Picot (multiple of 3 sts)

Cast on required number of stitches.

Rnds 1 - 5: Knit.

Rnd 6: [K1, yo, k2tog], repeat to end of rnd.

Rnds 7 - 11: Knit.

After your mitten is finished, fold the picot cuff at the k2tog rnd to the inside, and whip stitch the hem to the body of the mitten. inside, and whip stitch the hem to the body of the mitten.

Blocking

Many of the yarns used here are superwash, which means they've been treated chemically or physically to resist felting as they're worn. This is

useful when superwash yarns are used for socks (and shoved into shoes all day).

While mittens are often even nicer (read: *warmer*) if they are lightly felted, colorwork felts unpredictably thanks to the yarn floats on the wrong side of the fabric. Do NOT be tempted to felt the colorwork mittens unless you're prepared for potential disaster.

Instead, if you want to experiment with felted mittens, knit the liner mitten pattern Sigrun on page 20 in the largest size, in one color, in a heavier yarn weight such as worsted, then felt that by running it through a hot-then-cold cycle in your washing machine.

I will be releasing a video on knitgrrl.com for the pattern Fannar which shows you not only how to do this, but also how to embroider the resulting "overmitt" with a sharp yarn needle. You should always be able to find a link to the most current tutorial from its pattern page on Ravelry, here:

http://www.ravelry.com/patterns/library/fannar

For the *really* cold-blooded

Are you a complete freezebaby? There's no shame in having a luxurious knit liner like Sigrun, then a fancy colorwork mitten, then the felted mitten Fannar over top to keep you warm and dry in even the most challenging conditions. You might also want to knit the thrummed mittens Solveig. Christina Bowers, who spun the yarn and knit the sample, called them "hand ovens." They're *that* warm.

For texters

Love to text? Consider knitting the tip of your thumbs with conductive yarn. KnitPicks and other major retailers carry it: search for "conductive thread" or "conductive yarn." Some is designed to be knit as a carry-along, some are better suited for duplicate stitching into place after the fact for greater precision.

Wet blocking

When blocking these mittens, first weave in all the ends. Next, gently pull the mitten into shape if it's been deformed by stitch tension, and check for any gaps (in the thumb gusset area, at the top bind off, etc). Turn the mittens inside out and soak them until completely saturated in lukewarm water using Soak or your preferred wool wash.

Allow the mittens to soak for at least an hour (I often leave them in a bowl overnight), then lift them out and gently press out the excess water. Don't squeeze too hard! If you have access to your washing machine, you can also run them through the spin cycle to extract maximum liquid.

Turn the mittens right side out and lay flat to dry.

Permanent liners

If you're making lined mittens and want the two layers joined together permanently, leave the waste yarn in place on both mitten halves during the blocking process, allow them to dry thoroughly and then put the liners inside the mittens before binding off both pieces together as in a three-needle bindoff, or continuing to add an additional cuff section.

Skills required

These are common to all mittens in the book:

Knitting in the round

Following a chart

Increases/Decreases

Kitchener Stitch

Stranded knitting

I-cord cast on: see also the tutorial at: http://whimsicalknittingdesigns.blogspot.com/2006/10/i-cord-cast-on.html

Chart key

☐ No stitch

☐ MC

☐ CC

☐ K2tog

☐ Ssk

☐ K2tog in CC

☐ Ssk in CC

M Make 1

☐ Placement of right thumb gusset

☐ Placement of left thumb gusset

Techniques and how-to | 13

Color dominance

As previously mentioned, each pattern is knit in two colors, and many of the mittens have been knit both ways, i.e. one mitten is knit with MC as its motif color and CC as the background, while the other is knit with MC as background and CC as motif. It's a fast way to show you how very different the mittens will look if you choose to work them in one way or the other. You, of course, can pick your favorite and knit both mittens the same if you like.

In the photos here, Sindri has been knit with alternating MCs.

In addition, you should know that it is important to always carry your colors in the same way, i.e. with MC in the lower position if you carry both yarns in one hand, or always in your right hand if you knit with one color in each hand. Ysolda Teague has written a very thorough discussion of this topic here: http://ysolda.com/blog/2014/5/29/technique-thursday-colour-dominance

What she calls the "lower path" results in more yarn—a bigger stitch—being stretched across the space, so that color will be visually dominant. It really does make a difference! You may want to make a note of how you were holding your colors when you set your project down for the night (or for a longer rest). When we test knit the mitten patterns, the knitters returned them to us unblocked. Any switch in dominant color was even more glaring before blocking, and blocking doesn't even it out completely, so why take the risk?

Latvian Braid

I have a real love for Latvian design due to some Latvian childhood friends (and serious jealousy of their jewelry: search for "Latvian 7-day ring" and you'll see what I'm talking about). There's even a Viking connection to Latvia, believe it or not. Latvia's principle river, the Daugava, was part of the route between Norse territory down into Southern Europe and even the Middle East. See Astrid on page 63 for more about the trade routes and connections between north and south, or check out Lizbeth Upitis' book on Latvian mittens for even more mitten-related information. Iceland and the Norse countries were not the only source of some seriously amazing textile designs.

As for Latvian Braid, it's one of my favorite edgings, visually, and has been used in 2 places on Aslaug (seen at right) to frame the bottom motif. You can add the braid wherever you like to serve that purpose, even on other mittens in this collection.

Here's how to knit it (in the round):

R1: Knit around.

R2: Purl around.

R3: Knit 1 st in MC, then 1 st in CC; continue alternating colors to the end of the round.

R4: Bring both yarns to the front. You'll be purling the MC sts with the MC yarn and the CC sts with the CC yarn. The yarn that matches the next st on the LH needle will be held over the opposite yarn. The non-working yarn will hang in the front of the knitting.

- If your next st is MC, hold the MC yarn over the CC yarn and purl the next st with MC.
- If your next st is CC, hold the CC yarn over the MC yarn and purl the next st with CC.

Always purl the next st with the matching color (MC with MC, CC with CC). Continue in this manner to the end of the round.

R5: This row is similar to R4, but you're going to bring the working yarn under the non-working yarn for each st.

- f your next st is in MC, the MC will lie under the CC. The CC will hang in the front of the knitting. Purl the next st with MC.
- If your next st is in CC, the CC will lie under the MC. The MC will hang in front of the knitting. Purl the next st with CC.

As above, always purl the next st with the matching color. Work in pattern to the end of the round.

To reverse direction for the opposite mitten, simply reverse the way the yarn lies in R4 and R5. For R4 the yarn will lie under the non-working yarn. For R5 the yarn will lie over the non-working yarn.

Solveig

Sample knitter Christina Bowers said she not only wanted to demonstrate thrumming, but also spin the yarn for the mitten itself. Thrumming, a method of knitting unspun fiber into the stitches inside the mitten, creates a fluffy, cloud-like layer of air and wool that traps heat and keeps you extra warm. If you are a freezebaby, these mittens are for you! They're named after Solveig Gunbjørg Jacobsen, the first woman born in Antarctica. Christina calls them "hand ovens." They're *warm*.

Sizes

Women's S (M, L)

Finished Measurements

These will vary greatly based on the size and placement of your thrums. This basic pattern is similar to Sigrun, but you can thrum any of the mittens in this book if you like!

Materials

Malabrigo Nube spinning fiber for the handspun yarn, Cephalopod Yarns spinning fiber for the thrums (1.75 oz).

Stitch markers

Large-eyed, blunt sewing needle

Spinning info

This is how Christina spun the yarn seen here. "Malabrigo Nube was spun semi-woolen long forward draw into a dk/worsted single which I then chain plied. Yarn was soaked, thwacked to full the plies, then hung to dry. Weight: 4 oz. Yardage: 200 yds. Wanted even repeating semi-solid stripes, so the roving was split vertically along the entire length of roving before attenuating the fiber slightly to remove felted bits and open up dense areas."

Gauge

This will also vary greatly based on chosen yarns (or your handspun, if you choose to spin the main yarn, as Christina's done here).

Notes

How to thrum directions follow this pattern outline. Please be sure to read both the entire pattern and those directions before beginning.

Pattern

Cuff

Cast on 64 (72, 80) sts. Being careful not to twist, join to work in the round.

Work [k2, p2] cuff for 12 (14, 16) rnds.

Hand

Work each rnd in stockinette, until rnd 27 (18, 9).

Thumb Gusset

Next Rnd: Continue working in stockinette, placing a stitch marker either side of the first (right hand) or last (left hand) stitch on your second needle.

Try on your mitten. Gusset length is as individual as you are. You may want to add some extra rounds before separating the thumb sts, you may also want to add some extra increases. It all depends on your hands.

Once your thumb gusset is the length you want it, separate the thumb stitches from the hand as follows:

Work in stockinette to first stitch marker, place the thumb sts on waste yarn or a stitch holder, cast on one st, work to the end of the round.

Continue to work the hand in stockinette, until, when tried on, the mitten is 1" / 2.24cm shorter than desired.

Mitten Top

Rnd 1: [K1, ssk, k to 3 sts before end of needle, k2tog, k1], twice.

Repeat rnd 1 for 8 (10, 12) rnds, then kitchener stitch closed.

Thumb

Place your thumb sts back onto your needles, cast on 3 sts. - 22 (24, 26) sts.

Join to work in the round.

Work in stockinette until, when tried on, the thumb almost reaches the top of your thumb.

Rnd 1: [K2tog], across the rnd.

Repeat rnd 1.

Break yarn, and, with a sewing needle, thread yarn through remaining stitches, and pull tight.

Finishing

Weave in all ends, and wet block.

Thrumming

A How-to, Why-for, What-if Tutorial for Knitted Thrums by Christina Bowers

Thrums are lengths or sections of unspun fibers that lie parallel to each other and are mostly equal in length and width. They're typically used in knitted fabric for insulation and, depending on color, preparation, and distribution throughout the knitting, can create a lovely design that mimics the appearance of color work. Thrum width should match the weight of the yarn or be slightly thicker for insulation. The thicker the thrums, the thicker the mitten and the more you'll notice their pattern on the outside. Not too thick!

Thrums provide more insulation as you wear the knitted item because the friction of your skin against the thrums felts the fibers together over time creating an even warmer item. Texture + warmth + moisture = felt! Thrums are usually made using a non-superwash wool or other warm fibers such as: alpaca, cashmere or angora blended with wool (to minimize shedding), llama (for hard wearing knits), or any medium staple animal fiber that has the potential to felt together. The possibilities are endless as long as the staple length of the fiber is long enough to be manageable. Felting happens when the scales that cover and protect the individual fibers become agitated causing their ends to flare and interlock with each other. When this happens with a group of scaled fibers (animal, or protein, fibers) it makes felt.

Superwash fiber is not recommended because fibers processed this way have the scales removed using one of two methods: an acid bath that removes the scales or a polymer coating that prevents the scales from sticking out and felting together. You may use these fibers if you like, but a lot of the warmth will be sacrificed.

Directions for knitting thrums

Thrums can be made using any fiber preparation, but the simplest way is to use prepared roving (carded fibers that lie mostly parallel with some jumbled up fibers, less dense, more air between the fibers) or top (combed fibers that lie parallel to each other, very dense, compacted fibers). Thrums that are 2-4" (5-10 cm) work perfectly for mittens, but you may make yours whatever length you like, although thrums shorter than 2" (5 cm) will likely be very difficult to knit in and may not stay in place.

- Hold the roving or top in both hands with your hands placed several inches apart.

- Pull the roving or top apart by jerking your hands apart until you have several lengths of roving or top. You may do this slowly but the chances of achieving more equal lengths are a bit higher if you jerk them apart quickly. Sometimes, when pulling roving or top apart slowly, it will split in the middle and pull apart unevenly. Play around to find your comfort zone.

- Take one section of roving/top and pull strips off the roving that are .15-.75" (.38-1.9cm) thick. You'll want it to be a similar thickness to the yarn you're using. Continue pulling off strips until you have a big pile of thrums of relatively the same size. The number of strips you get from each section depends on how thick the roving or top is and how thick you want your thrums to be. Twist each thrum a few times to make them easier to knit along with your yarn.

- When you come to the point in the pattern where you need to add a thrum simply hold the thrum along with the yarn and knit the thrum along with the next knitted stitch. Make sure that when you knit the thrum, you are knitting the middle section so your thrums are evenly spaced and do not fall or pull out of the knitting. To do this you may lie the thrum over the yarn and the finger you use to throw the yarn to knit the thrum together with the yarn. If you pick the yarn continental style, you may simply hold the thrum parallel to your working yarn so that the middle of the thrum will line up with your next stitch, allowing you to grab the yarn with the thrum. The thrums in the handspun sample were knit in a basic allover 3:1 pattern as follows:

- R1: *K1 with thrum, K3 plain* to end.
- R2: Knit
- R3: K2, *K1 with thrum, K3; con't from * to end.
- R4: Knit.
- Repeat for entire length of mitten or use a pattern of your choosing.
- If the thrum looks wonky, you can unknit it and try again or simply adjust it slightly as you go or after the knitting is complete. While you knit it's convenient to gently brush the thrums toward the middle of the mitten and down toward the cuff so they don't get in the way of following rounds.

What if...?

What if I want my thrums to make a pattern on the outside of the mitten? What if I'm allergic to wool? What if I don't want to use roving?

If you'd like your thrums to make a different pattern on the outside of the mitten, simply knit them in the pattern you'd like by holding them along with the yarn as instructed. You can knit them into any design, but I recommend keeping it simple as thrums are chunkier and will most likely hide any fine detail as they become felted. Make a basic chart for yourself to follow as you knit and experiment with allover patterns.

If you are allergic to wool, a non-wool substitute such as alpaca would add a wonderful amount of warmth as alpaca is three times warmer than wool. It's also softer than a lot of medium wools used for felting. Alpaca will not felt as well as some wools, but it will somewhat for a cozy layer. You could also use another fiber from the Camelid family, as people with wool allergies often will not have reactions to these luxurious fibers.

If you don't want to use roving or you have other fiber preparations on hand that you'd prefer to use, you can card or comb fibers from batts, cleaned fleeces, locks, or even punis or thin rolags that have been pulled apart for shorter lengths. Locks, single or pulled from a freshly cleaned fleece, would make for fun texture and be an interesting talking point. Experiment!

When you're done with your thrummed mittens you will have what feels like pleasantly warm and cozy hand ovens. Bring it on, winter!

Sigrun

SHANNON'S FRIEND AND FELLOW COOPERATIVE PRESS author Kate Atherley is always cold. *Always*. She suffers through each frigid Toronto winter layered like a woolen pan of lasagna. Sigrun is designed for the Kates of the world: these mitten liners can be paired with any other pair in the book for an extra layer of warmth. Wool and cashmere yarn was used for this pair; consider wool-silk blends, too. The name Sigrun means 'secret victory,' and is the name of a Valkyrie. Consider these your secret victory over the cold of winter!

Sizes

Women's S (M, L)

Finished Measurements

8 (9, 10)" / 20.32 (22.86, 25.4)cm circumference

7.8 (9, 10)" / 19.81 (22.86, 25.4)cm tall without cuff

Materials

KFI Cash Fine yarn [70% extra fine merino wool, 30% cashmere; 355 yds / 108m per 50g skein]; color: Natural;

1 set US #1/2.25 mm needles, or size needed to obtain gauge. Choose needles for knitting in the round over a small circumference: dpns, two circulars, or one long circular for magic loop, as you prefer.

Waste yarn or stitch holder for thumb stitches

Stitch markers

Large-eyed, blunt sewing needle

Gauge

32 sts x 36 rnds = 4"/10cm square in stitch pattern.

Notes

This is a generically shaped Liner Mitten. To make a liner that precisely matches your colorwork mitten, follow the directions for that mitten, working in plain stockinette. To make a slightly smaller, more densely fabriced mitten, go down a needle size.

Pattern

Cuff

Cast on 64 (72, 80) sts. Being careful not to twist, join to work in the round.

Work [k2, p2] cuff for 12 (14, 16) rnds.

Hand

Work each rnd in stockinette, until rnd 27 (18, 9).

Thumb Gusset

Next Rnd: Continue working in stockinette, placing a stitch marker either side of the first (right hand) or last (left hand) stitch on your second needle.

Try on your mitten. Gusset length is as individual as you are. You may want to add some extra rounds before separating the thumb sts, you may also want to add some extra increases. It all depends on your hands.

Once your thumb gusset is the length you want it, separate the thumb stitches from the hand as follows:

Work in stockinette to first stitch marker, place the thumb sts on waste yarn or a stitch holder, cast on one st, work to the end of the round.

Continue to work the hand in stockinette, until, when tried on, the mitten is 1" / 2.24cm shorter than desired.

Mitten Top

Rnd 1: [K1, ssk, k to 3 sts before end of needle, k2tog, k1], twice.

Repeat rnd 1 for 8 (10, 12) rnds, then kitchener stitch closed.

Thumb

Place your thumb sts back onto your needles, cast on 3 sts. - 22 (24, 26) sts.

Join to work in the round.

Work in stockinette until, when tried on, the thumb almost reaches the top of your thumb.

Rnd 1: [K2tog], across the rnd.

Repeat rnd 1.

Break yarn, and, with a sewing needle, thread yarn through remaining stitches, and pull tight.

Finishing

Weave in all ends, and wet block.

Fannar

Another one for the freezebabies, Fannar is a name derived from the Old Norse word *fönn*, which means 'snow drift.' This mitten uses one of my favorite techniques for blocking wind, snow and cold: knitting then fulling (*felting*), and adding form-fitting rib after the fact. You can leave these plain and wear them with a liner (or another pair of mittens), or embroider them with a sharp yarn needle, as suggested here.

Sizes

Adjustable based on directions.

Finished Measurements

These will vary wildly depending on multiple variables. I will address this in the directions.

Materials

You will need cotton dishcloth or another non-felting yarn to use as waste yarn in your cast on (just a yard or two). For the main body of the mitten, I've chosen Cascade 220 yarn in a marled heather colorway.

Any non-superwash yarn that felts will work. Please note that while this is technically "fulling," I am using the more commonly-used term "felting" throughout. I have found with extensive experience that Cascade 220 felts into a smoother and more easily-controlled fabric than many other yarns. If you don't want to embroider on the mittens, and would prefer a "furry" surface, I recommend Brown Sheep's yarn Lamb's Pride, which has a small amount of mohair in its single ply structure that ends up puffing from the surface post-felting in an attractive way.

Want more information, including video? See this pattern's Ravelry page for links to all video content:

http://www.ravelry.com/patterns/library/fannar

Pattern

Follow the directions for the largest size of the Sigrun mitten pattern (page 20) unless you have extremely small hands or are knitting these for a child.

Cast on using the long tail provisional cast on method and dishcloth cotton. You may need to adjust how you are holding the two strands of yarn if the wool yarn is not ending up as stitches on the needle. (The cotton yarn will "weave" between the stitches below your needle as you cast on). Discard the initial cast on slipknot, it does not count as a stitch) before checking your cast on count and joining the first round.

Knit the mittens. Keep in mind that they will shrink more vertically than horizontally, so ideally, your mittens will end up only a bit wider than your hand and about 1.5 times as tall as the length between your cuff area and the top of your tallest finger.

Knit-Shrink Felting

Felting is fun! It is also unpredictable. The easiest way to do it is in a top-loading washer. If you have a front loader, or if you are going to felt by hand (rubbing the mitten fabric under alternating hot and cold water), you may want to knit and felt a swatch first and process it accordingly to check the amount your chosen yarn felts. Be sure to mark the cast on edge with a twist tie or a piece of yarn so you can tell which side is up after it shrinks!

Please don't fall for any online felting directions that tell you to add tennis balls, old tennis shoes or towels into your washing machine to felt it "faster." Not unless you really, *really* like picking pieces of terrycloth towel or neon yellow tennis ball fuzz out of felted fabric...you don't.

Choose a low water fill option for your washer, and the hottest, roughest cycle available, followed by cold rinse. On my washer, it's the "heavy duty" cycle, hot wash/cold rinse.

When felting, it's important to quickly transition between hot and cold because the three factors that most heavily affect felting are temperature, water Ph (changed with soap) and agitation/friction, which is provided by the washer itself. (Or your hands, if you're felting manually in the sink. If so, wear rubber dish gloves, your hands will thank you later!)

Add laundry detergent or soap. If you've had problems getting items to felt previously, you may want to skip the detergent and add plain old dish soap. Dawn is my preferred dish soap because it also strips off any lingering oils from wool processing that keep yarns from felting quickly.

Add the mittens and allow the washer cycle to start. If you're new to felting, you may want to periodically open the washer and pull out a mitten to check if the felting process has started. I suggest letting it run for at least 5 minutes before your first check.

What you want is for the individual stitches to "melt together" and become a solid fabric. Some yarns take longer than others. The water that is absorbed into the mitten will make it seem heavy; don't be shy! Pull on the mitten if you need to in order to check the fabric status, it can be tougher to see if it's done with darker colored yarns. If it's still fairly "floppy," put it back in and keep going. If it seems harder, and the mitten is already smaller, you may want to skip ahead to the cold rinse cycle by manipulating your washer's controls.

Allow your washer to spin out excess water at the end, but be careful not to let the mittens get stuck under the center agitator or otherwise deformed. Sometimes the ends of your dishcloth cotton waste yarn will catch on things!

Wool naturally sheds water, and felting blocks penetrating winds. Sheep are comfy outside even on the coldest days and you can be, too!

Remove the mitten and place it flat on the top of your washer. Check sizing by putting your hand on top -- you should have a bit of extra fabric around the sides and top of your hand, especially if you plan to wear the felted mitten as an "overmitten" to a liner or another pair of mittens.

Still a little big? Stitches still excessively visible? Put the mitten in your dryer on a hot (cotton) cycle. Check every 10 minutes. This will often provide the last little bit of "tightening" needed for the fabric. Allow to dry flat.

Finishing

You can leave the mitten as is! For funky fuzzy yarns such as Lamb's Pride, or to even out the texture on Cascade 220, use a hairbrush to align the loose fibers on the surface. Brush hard, and resist the urge to use a sweater shaver or similar instrument, it makes the fabric spiky and uncomfortable.

If you plan to embroider the surface of your mitten, do it before you add the cuffs. Get a sharp-tipped yarn needle and yarn colors of your choice. Sublime Stitching (sublimestitching.com) has some great free PDF patterns to give you ideas, or stick to simple patterns like flowers. Tailor's chalk or disappearing markers meant for sewing are a good way to plan out a pattern on your surface that can be removed later. Honestly, even the simplest stitched stripes or geometric patterns are fun and anyone can do them!

After you're happy with the mitten surface, pick out the cotton waste yarn and place the live stitches back onto an appropriately-sized circular needle or DPNs. Using wool (either the original mitten color or a contrast), knit 1x1 ribbing for as long as you like then bind off. (Cast on an additional stitch if your cast on number is not even for some reason). You can also bind off immediately with the working yarn for a braid-like outer edge.

Thora

These mittens are named after a specific Thora: Þóra Borgarhjörtr, one of Ragnar Loðbrók's three wives. Ragnar, who you may know from History Channel's excellent series *Vikings*, was actually a historical figure, and married to one of my foremothers. The spiky thistle flower in the pattern represents the dragon lurking in the overgrowth surrounding Thora's bower before Ragnar slew him and married Thora. Read more in the story *Ragnarssona þáttr*, linked in Sources, page 106.

Sizes

Women's (M, L)

Finished Measurements

9.75 (11.25)" / 24.76 (28.58)cm circumference

9.5 (10.5)" / 24.13 (26.67)cm high without cuff

Materials

Knit Picks Palette yarn [100% Peruvian highland wool; 231 yds / 211m per 50g skein]; colors: Caper and Chicory.

1 set US #1/2.25 mm needles, or size needed to obtain gauge. Choose needles for knitting in the round over a small circumference: dpns, two circulars, or one long circular for magic loop, as you prefer.

Waste yarn or stitch holder for thumb stitches

Stitch markers

Large-eyed, blunt sewing needle

Gauge

32 sts x 36 rnds = 4"/10cm square in stitch pattern.

Notes

Work the stitches inside the red rectangle for medium size.

If you are working the largest size, work all the stitches.

The red solid square is for medium thumb gusset placement.

The green solid square is for large thumb gusset placement.

Hands, however, are as unique as you are. Try on your mitten, you may need to move the gusset start up or down a few rounds.

Pattern

Cuff

Cast on 78 (90) sts. Being careful not to twist, join to work in the round.

Work the cuff of your choice, as described on page 11.

Hand

Using chart A for the back of hand, and Chart B for the palm, work as follows:

Medium: Work the stitches within both red rectangles.

Large: Work the whole chart.

Work as set, until rnd 18 (9).

Thumb Gusset

All sizes

Left hand: Place a stitch marker either side of the color coded stitch for your size on the right hand side of

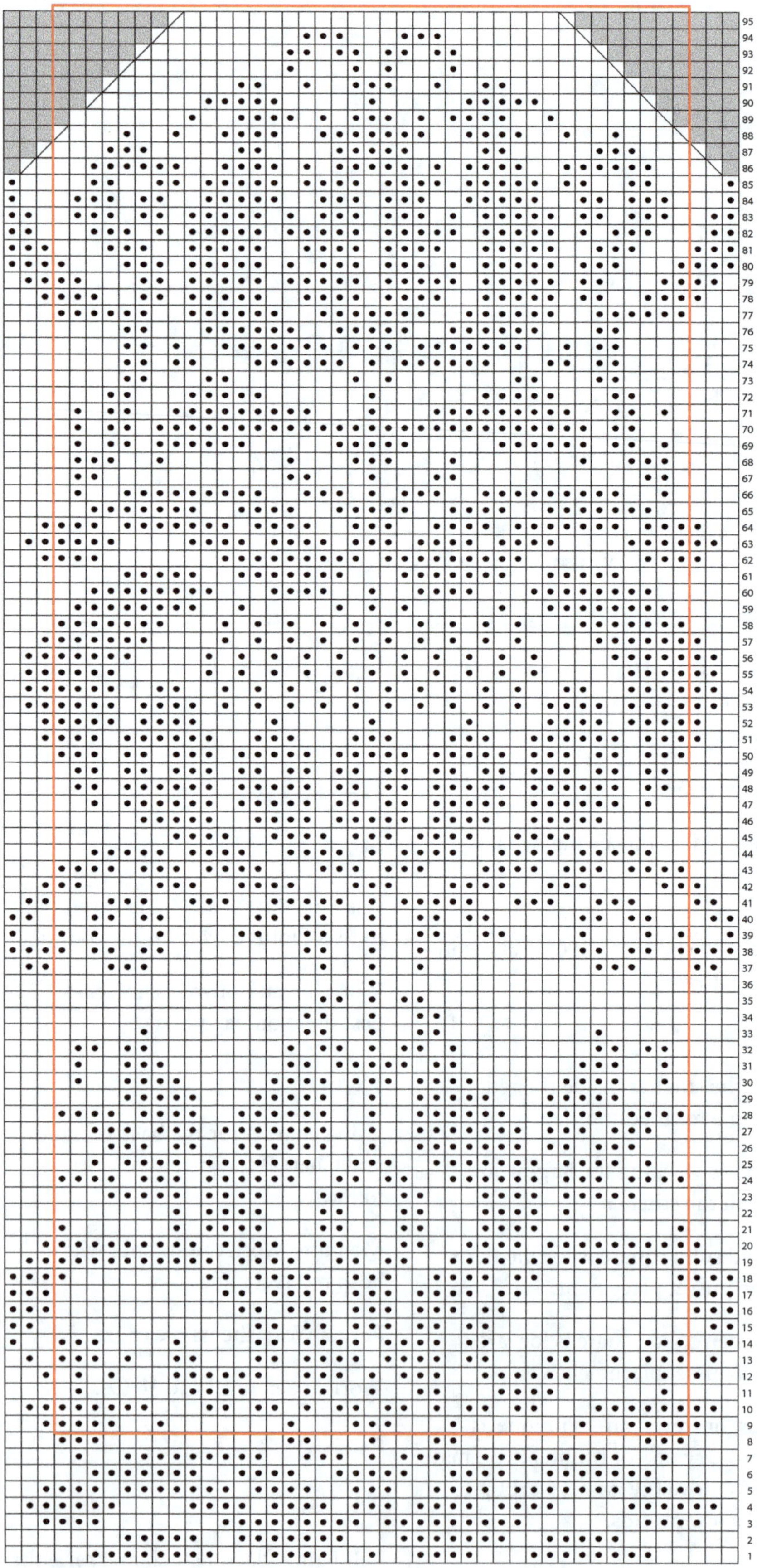

Aurora Borealis Mittens | 28

your rectangle. Work the gusset chart between the stitch markers.

Right hand: Place a stitch marker either side of the color coded square for your size on the left hand side of your rectangle. Work the gusset chart between the stitch markers.

Work the hand charts as set until all increases have been completed.

Try on your mitten. Gusset length is as individual as you are. You may want to add some extra rounds before separating the thumb sts, you may also want to add some extra increases. It all depends on your hands. If you are adding extra rounds, just continue your thumb stitch pattern as set.

Once your thumb gusset is the length you want it, divide for the thumb as follows:

Work in pattern to first stitch marker, place the thumb sts on waste yarn or a stitch holder, cast on one st, work to the end of the round.

Continue to work the hand charts, as set until the last round is completed.

Break CC, and with MC, kitchener stitch the hand closed.

Thumb

Place your thumb sts back onto your needles, cast on 3 sts. - 24 (26) sts.

Work the appropriate thumb chart. Break CC, with MC, kitchener stitch the thumb closed.

Stranded colorwork thumbs tend to be narrower than you'd expect. Try working your thumb with MC only, and use a duplicate stitch in CC for your stitch pattern after the thumb is completed.

Finishing

Weave in all ends, and wet block.

CHART A

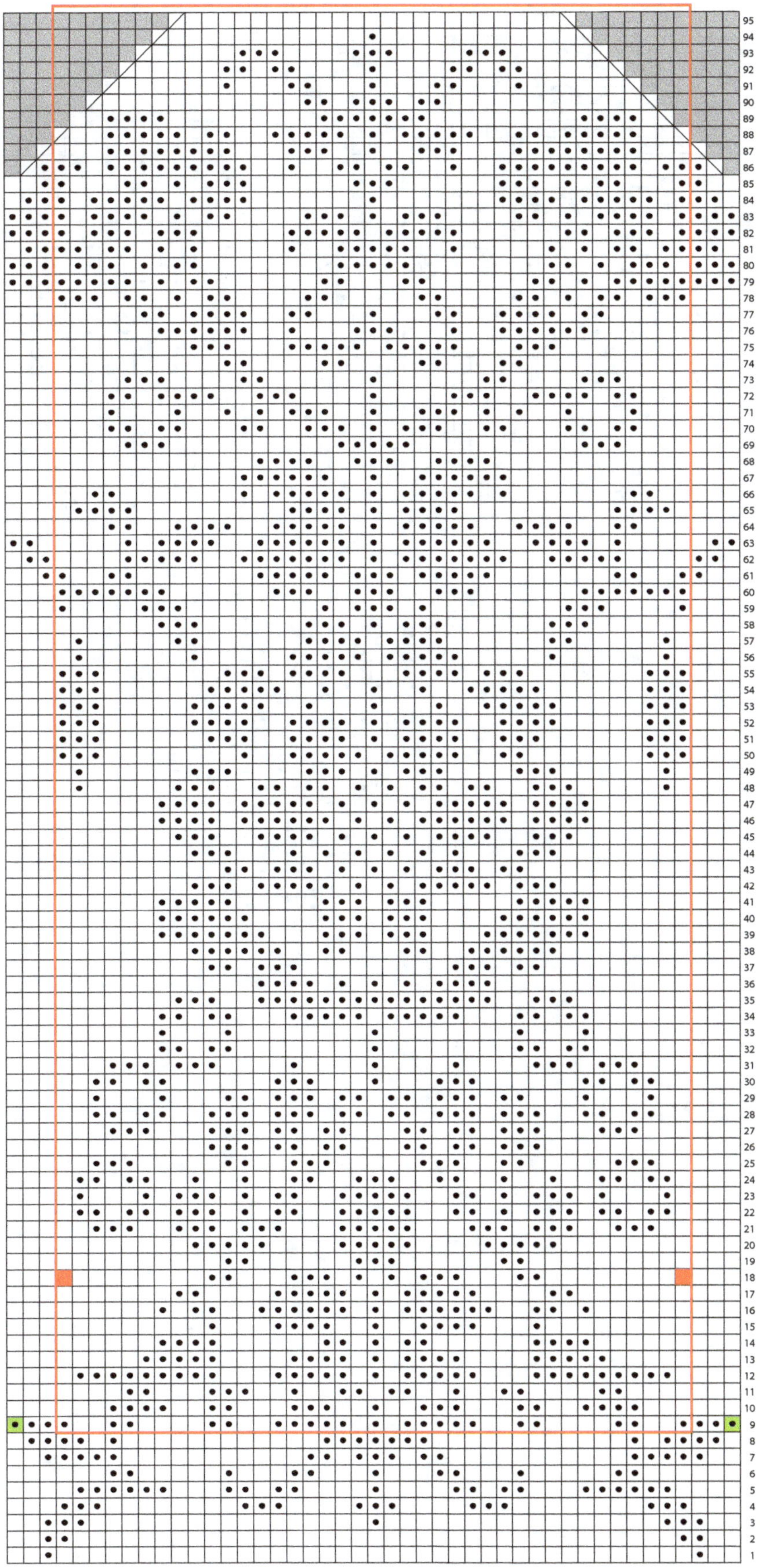

Thora | 29

CHART B

Aurora Borealis Mittens | 30

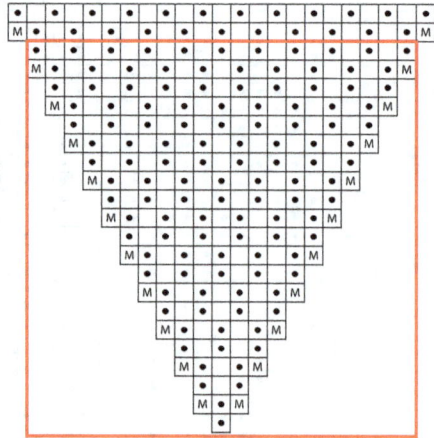

THUMB

Sample knitter Marie Duquette tests out the fruits of her knitting labor. Note the cuff hasn't been added yet, and the provisional cast on is still in place.

Nordic Stars

As you'll learn in the introduction to Aud, there was a considerable amount of travel and cross-cultural communication among the Norse and northernmost Celtic peoples. Shetland is almost as close to Oslo as it is geographically to Glasgow. The jarls who ruled Orkney for years were all Norse. Knitters in the Nordic world created their textiles under the same broad swath of stars in the sky, hence these mitten's name.

Sizes

Women's S (M, L)

Yellow/brown pair shown in Large, with Cuff Option 1

Green/blue/black pair shown in Large, with Cuff Option 1 and 6

Finished Measurements

8.25 (9.75, 11.25)" / 20.95 (24.76, 28.58)cm circumference

7.7 (8.7, 10)" / 19.56 (22.1, 25.4)cm high without cuff

Materials

(yellow and brown pair) Knit Picks Palette yarn [100% Peruvian highland wool; 231 yds / 211m per 50g skein]; colors: Serpentine and Wallaby.

(green, blue and black pair) Blue Moon Fiber Arts Socks That Rock Lightweight yarn [100% superwash merino wool; 405 yds / 370m per 146g skein]; colors: Waltzing Lobelia (multi), Thraven (black);

1 set US #1/2.25 mm needles, or size needed to obtain gauge. Choose needles for knitting in the round over a small circumference: dpns, two circulars, or one long circular for magic loop, as you prefer.

Waste yarn or stitch holder for thumb stitches

Stitch markers

Large-eyed, blunt sewing needle

Gauge

32 sts x 36 rnds = 4"/10cm square in stitch pattern.

Notes

Work the stitches inside the blue rectangle for small size.

Work the stitches inside the red rectangle for medium size.

If you are working the largest size, work all the stitches.

The blue solid square is for small thumb gusset placement.

The red solid square is for medium thumb gusset placement.

The green solid square is for large thumb gusset placement.

Hands, however, are as unique as you are. Try on your mitten, you may need to move the gusset start up or down a few rounds.

Pattern

Cuff

Cast on 66 (78, 90) sts. Being careful not to twist, join to work in the round.

Work the cuff of your choice, as described on page 11.

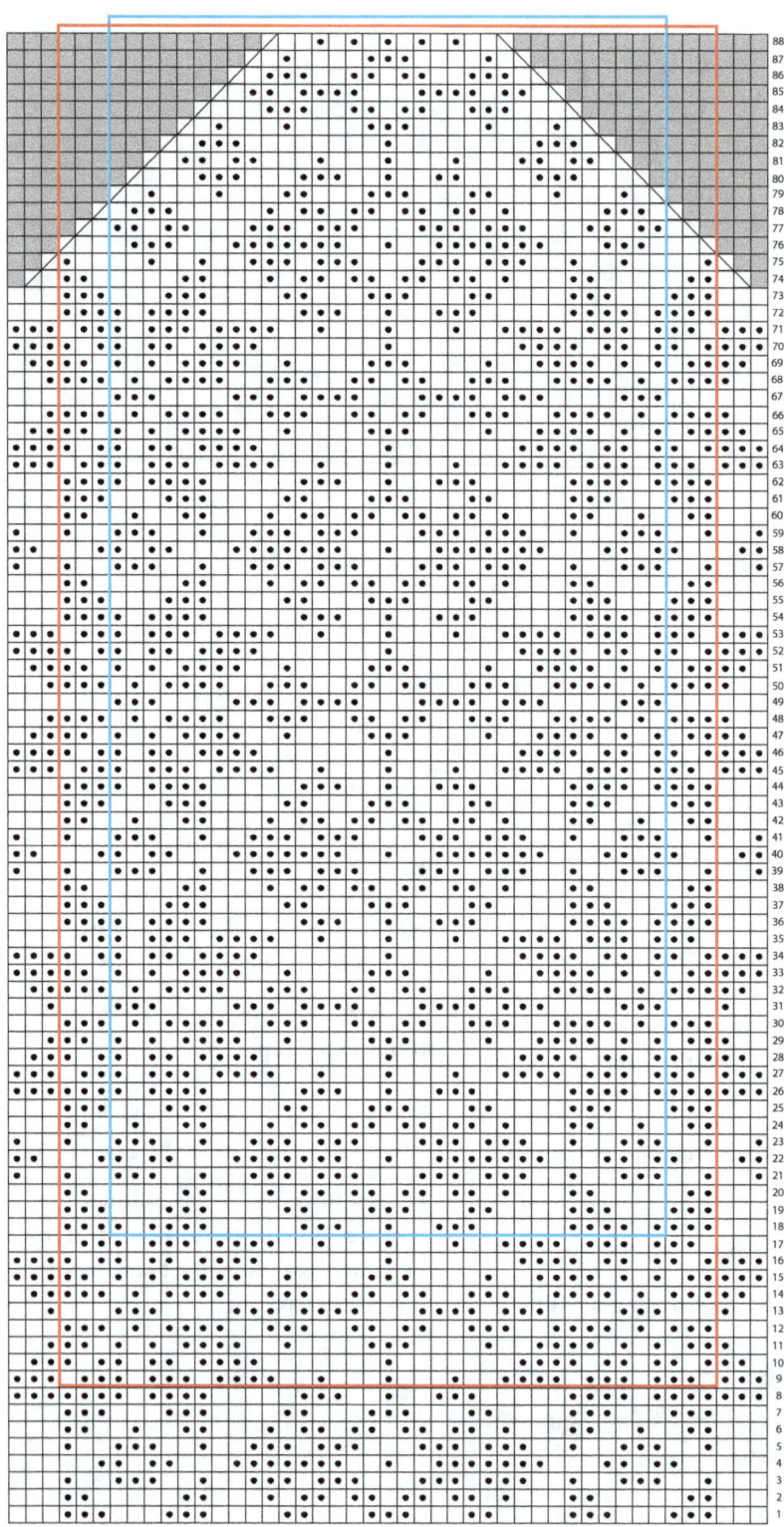

CHART A

Hand

Using chart A for the back of hand, and Chart B for the palm, work as follows:

Small: Work the stitches within both blue rectangles.

Medium: Work the stitches within both red rectangles.

Large: Work the whole chart.

Work as set, until rnd 27 (18, 9).

Thumb Gusset

All sizes

Left hand: Place a stitch marker either side of the color coded stitch for your size on the right hand side of your rectangle. Work the gusset chart between the stitch markers.

Right hand: Place a stitch marker either side of the color coded square for your size on the left hand side of your rectangle. Work the gusset chart between the stitch markers.

Work the hand charts as set until all increases have been completed.

Try on your mitten. Gusset length is as individual as you are. You may want to add some extra rounds before separating the thumb sts, you may also want to add some extra increases. It all depends on your hands. If you are adding extra rounds,

just continue your thumb stitch pattern as set.

Once your thumb gusset is the length you want it, divide for the thumb as follows:

Work in pattern to first stitch marker, place the thumb sts on waste yarn or

Nordic Stars | 35

a stitch holder, cast on one st, work to the end of the round.

Continue to work the hand charts, as set until the last round is completed.

Break CC, and with MC, kitchener stitch the hand closed.

Thumb

Place your thumb sts back onto your needles, cast on 3 sts. - 22 (24, 26) sts.

Work the appropriate thumb chart. Break CC, with MC, kitchener stitch the thumb closed.

Stranded colorwork thumbs tend to be narrower than you'd expect. Try working your thumb with MC only, and use a duplicate stitch in CC for your stitch pattern after the thumb is completed.

Finishing

Weave in all ends, and wet block.

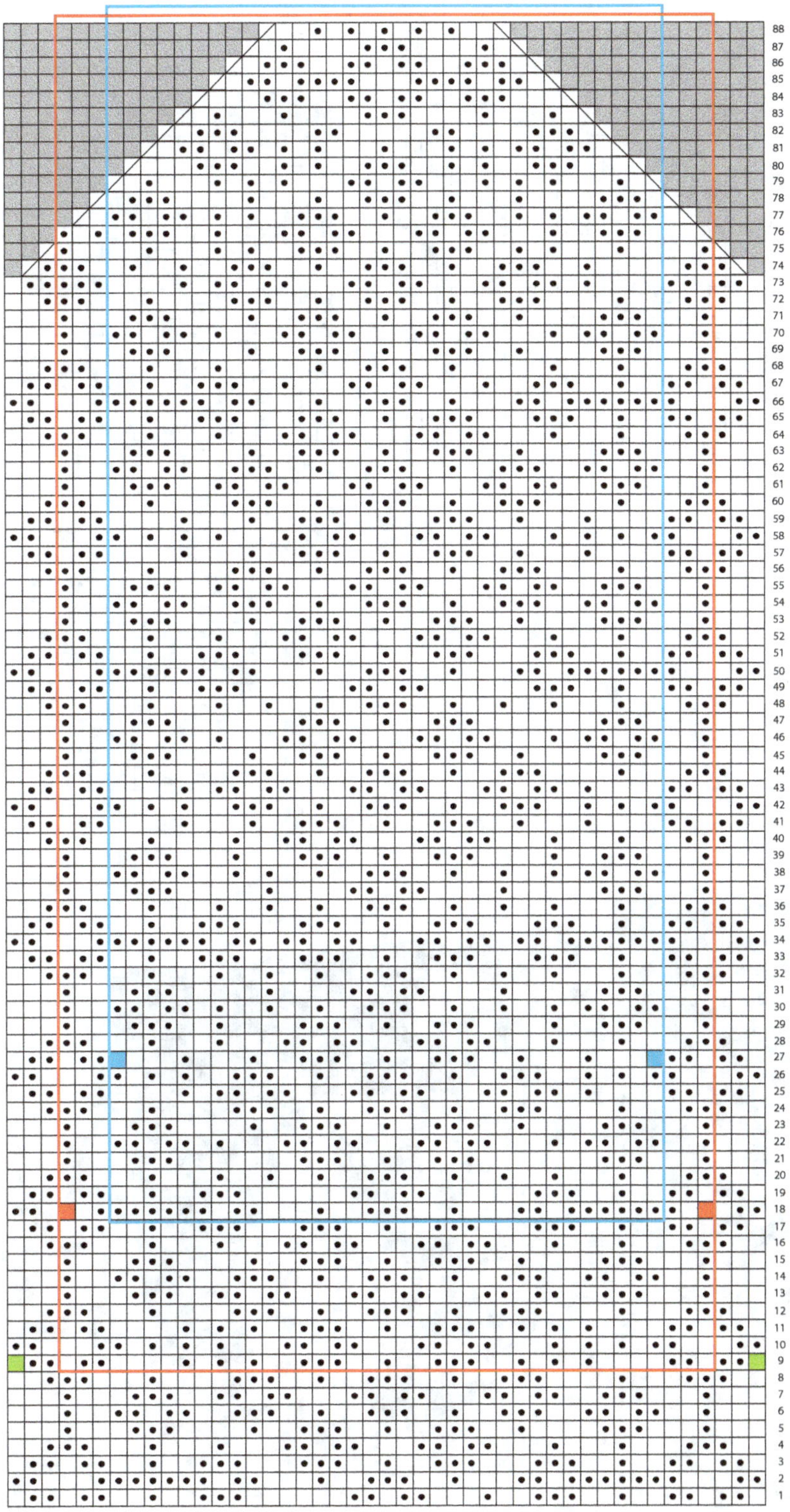

CUFF DETAIL

CHART B

Aurora Borealis Mittens | 36

THUMB

"Celtic Heart," the working name for these mittens, alludes to the family ties of Aud the Deep-Minded, one of Iceland's first settlers. Married to the King of Dublin, she later sailed to Orkney to marry off her granddaughter before leaving for Iceland. Icelandic DNA, some of the most closely-studied in the world due to its homogeneity, is almost 70% Celtic in the maternal line, while the male line is thoroughly Norse. Some might say this is because the Vikings kidnapped a large number of Irish women, but others believe they left of their own volition. Vikings were quite fashionably dressed and well-groomed compared to what they'd left behind! There's something to be said for bathing more than once a year.

Sizes

Women's M (L); shown in size L

Finished Measurements

8 (9.5)" / 20.32 (24.13) cm circumference.

9 (10.5)" / 22.36 (26.29) cm tall without cuff.

Materials

Freia Fibers Flux Fingering yarn [75% wool, 25% nylon; 196 yds / 215m per 50g skein]; color: Metal Earth;

Freia Fibers Semi Solids sock yarn [75% wool, 25% nylon; 196 yds / 215m per 50g skein]; color: Blue Patina;

1 set US #1/2.25 mm needles, or size needed to obtain gauge. Choose needles for knitting in the round over a small circumference: dpns, two circulars, or one long circular for magic loop, as you prefer.

Waste yarn or stitch holder for thumb stitches

Stitch markers

Large-eyed, blunt sewing needle

Gauge

32 sts x 36 rnds = 4"/10cm square in stitch pattern.

Notes

Work the stitches inside the red rectangle for medium size. If you are working the largest size, work all the stitches.

The red solid square is for medium thumb gusset placement.

The green solid square is for large thumb gusset placement.

Hands, however, are as unique as you are. Try on your mitten, you may need to move the gusset start up or down a few rounds.

Pattern

Cuff

Cast on 62 (74) sts. Being careful not to twist, join to work in the round.

Work the cuff of your choice, as described on page 11.

Aurora Borealis Mittens | 40

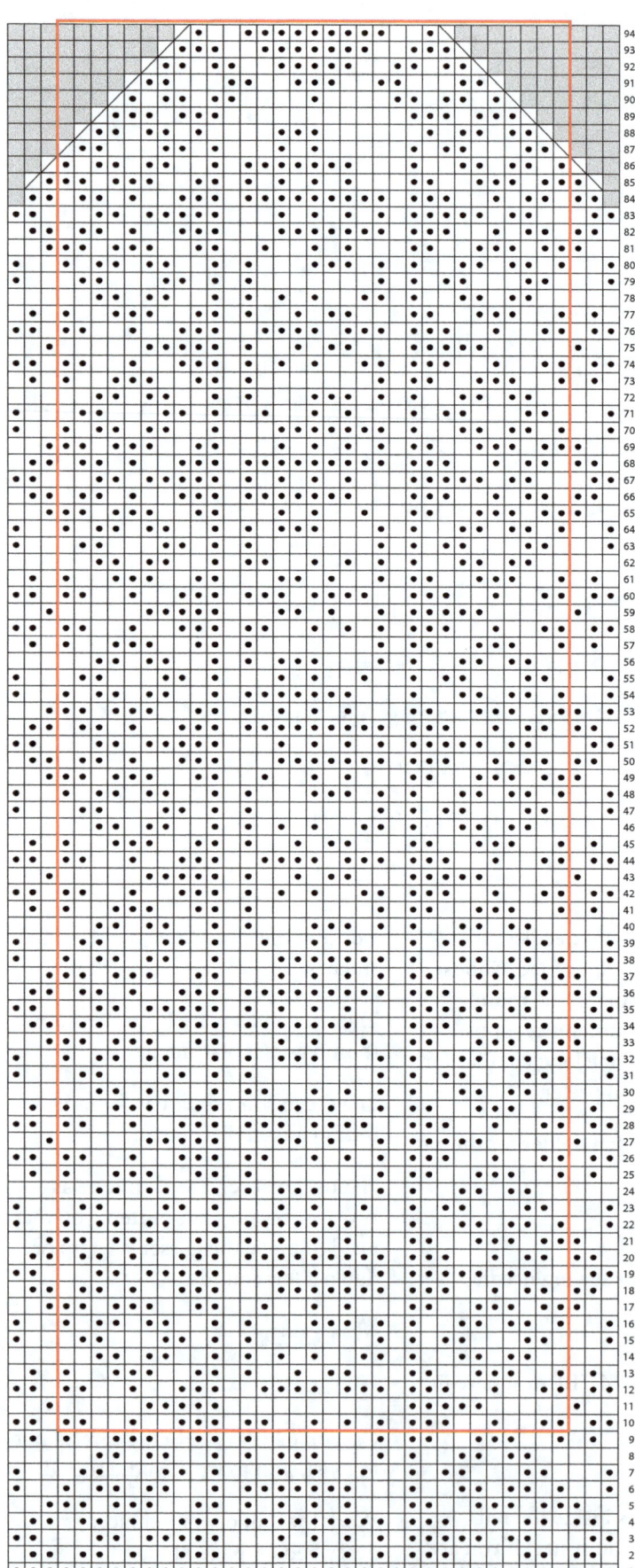

CHART A

Hand

Using chart A for the back of hand, and Chart B for the palm, work as follows:

Medium: Work the stitches from both red rectangles.

Large: Work the whole chart.

Work as set, until rnd 18 (9).

Thumb Gusset

All sizes

Left hand: Place a stitch marker either side of the color coded stitch for your size on the right hand side of your rectangle. Work the gusset chart between the stitch markers.

Right hand: Place a stitch marker either side of the color coded square for your size on the left hand side of your rectangle. Work the gusset chart between the stitch markers.

Work the hand charts as set until all increases have been completed.

Try on your mitten. Gusset length is as individual as you are. You may want to add some extra rounds before separating the thumb sts, you may also want to add some extra increases. It all depends on your hands. If you are adding extra rounds, just continue your thumb stitch pattern as set.

Once your thumb gusset is the length you want it, divide for the thumb as follows:

Work in pattern to first stitch marker, place the thumb sts on waste yarn or a stitch holder, cast on one st, work to the end of the round.

Continue to work the hand charts, as set until the last round is completed.

Break CC, and with MC, kitchener stitch the hand closed.

Thumb

Place your thumb sts back onto your needles, cast on 3 sts. - 22 (24, 26) sts.

Work the appropriate thumb chart. Break CC, with MC, kitchener stitch the thumb closed.

Stranded colorwork thumbs tend to be narrower than you'd expect. Try working your thumb with MC only, and use a duplicate stitch in CC for your stitch pattern after the thumb is completed.

Finishing

Weave in all ends, and wet block.

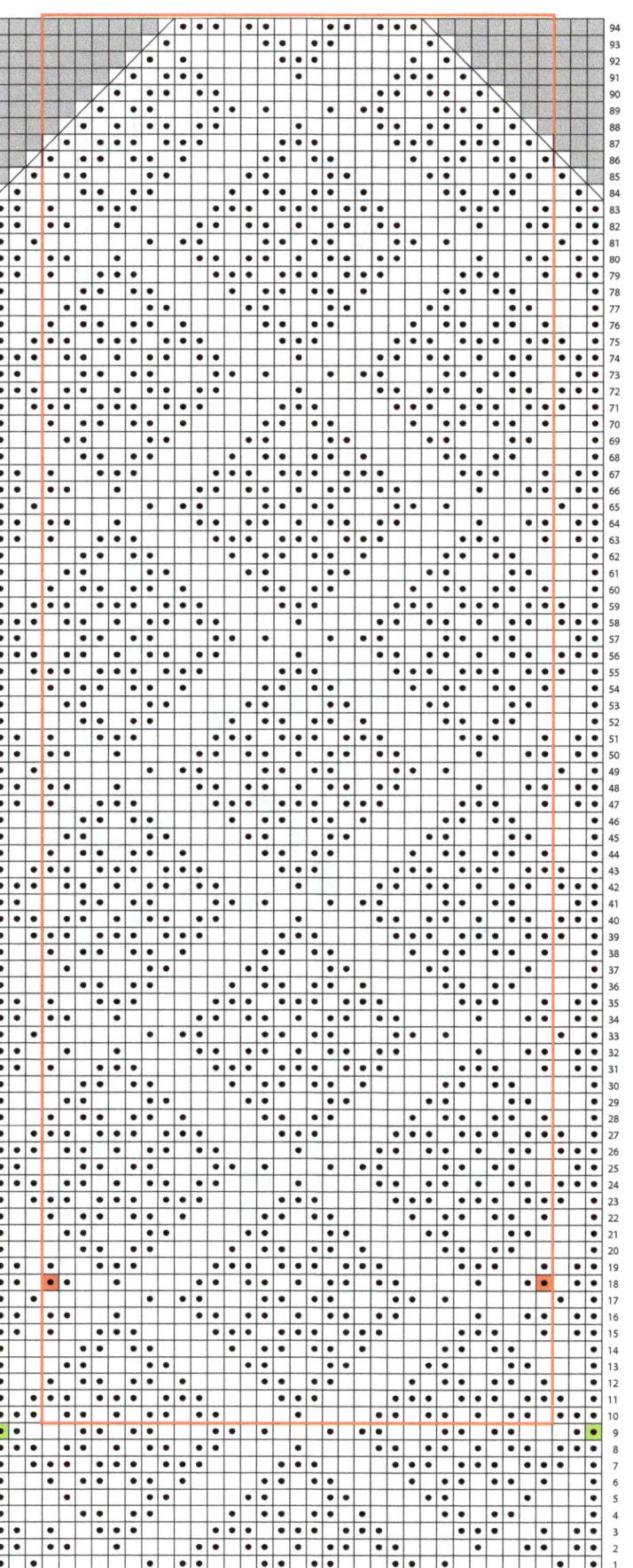

CHART B

Aurora Borealis Mittens | 42

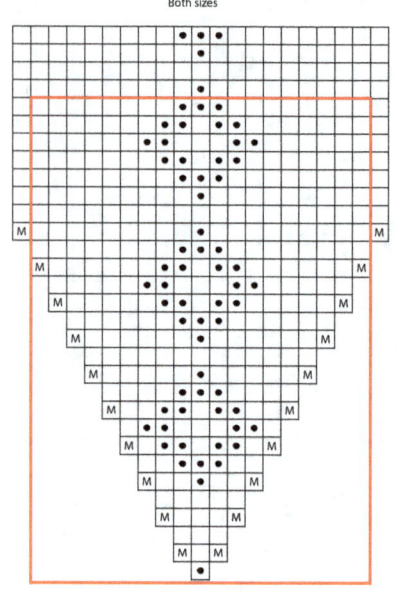

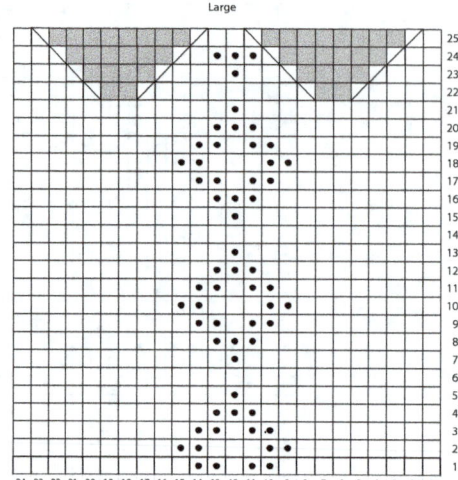

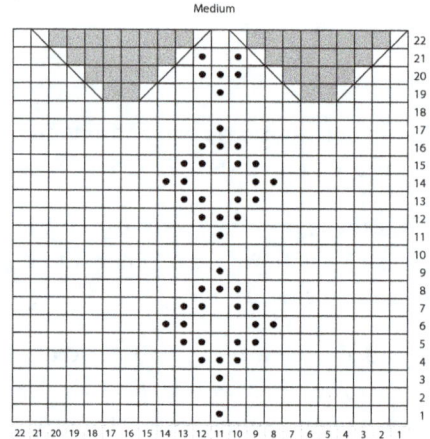

Thumb

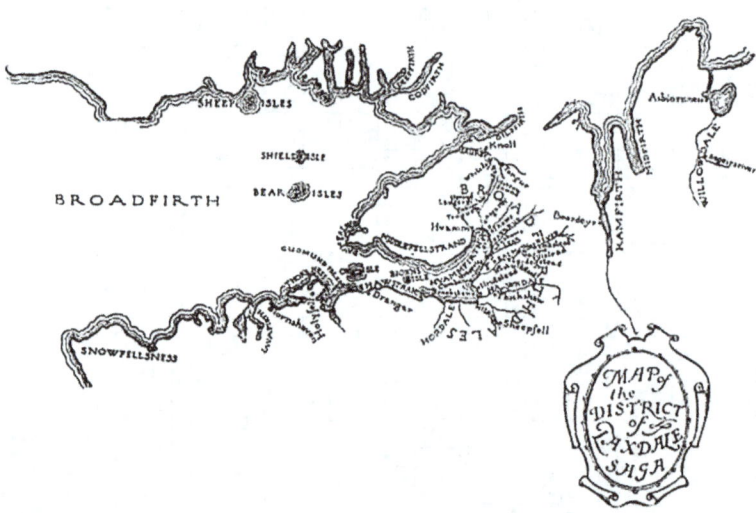

This is a map from an 1899 Laxdæla Saga translation showing the lands involved, including Aud's (she is referred to as Unn in this particular translation). You can read it for free online at Project Gutenberg (http://www.gutenberg.org)!

Halldora

When I designed these mittens I was not actually thinking about Halldora (whose story happens to be part of a saga related to another Gudrid) but Gudrid the Far Traveller, who made it all the way to Vinland in North America. So many of the names get repeated in these sagas that they all start to blur together after a while! I opted to name these Halldora instead, and prevent Gudrid-overload.

Sizes

Women's S (M, L)

Main picture shown in Large, with Cuff Option 2 and 3

Secondary picture shown in large, with Cuff Option 3

Finished Measurements

7.75 (9.25, 10.75)" / 19.68 (23.49, 27.3)cm circumference

7.8 (9, 10)" / 19.81 (22.86, 25.4)cm high without cuff

Materials

Teal and white pair: Knit Picks Palette yarn [100% Peruvian highland wool; 231 yds / 211m per 50g skein]; colors: Shoal and Finnley Heather.

Yellow and grey pair: Quince & Co Finch yarn [100% American wool; 221 yds / 202m per 50g skein]; colors: Honey and Kumlien's Gull;

1 set US #1/2.25 mm needles, or size needed to obtain gauge. Choose needles for knitting in the round over a small circumference: dpns, two circulars, or one long circular for magic loop, as you prefer.

Waste yarn or stitch holder for thumb stitches

Stitch markers

Large-eyed, blunt sewing needle

Gauge

32 sts x 36 rnds = 4"/10cm square in stitch pattern.

Notes

Work the stitches inside the blue rectangle for small size

Work the stitches inside the red rectangle for medium size.

If you are working the largest size, work all the stitches.

The blue solid square is for small thumb gusset placement.

The red solid square is for medium thumb gusset placement.

The green solid square is for large thumb gusset placement.

Hands, however, are as unique as you are. Try on your mitten, you may need to move the gusset start up or down a few rounds.

Pattern

Cuff

Cast on 62 (74, 86) sts. Being careful not to twist, join to work in the round.

Work the cuff of your choice, as described on page 11.

Hand

Using chart A for the back of hand, and Chart B for the palm, work as follows:

Aurora Borealis Mittens | 46

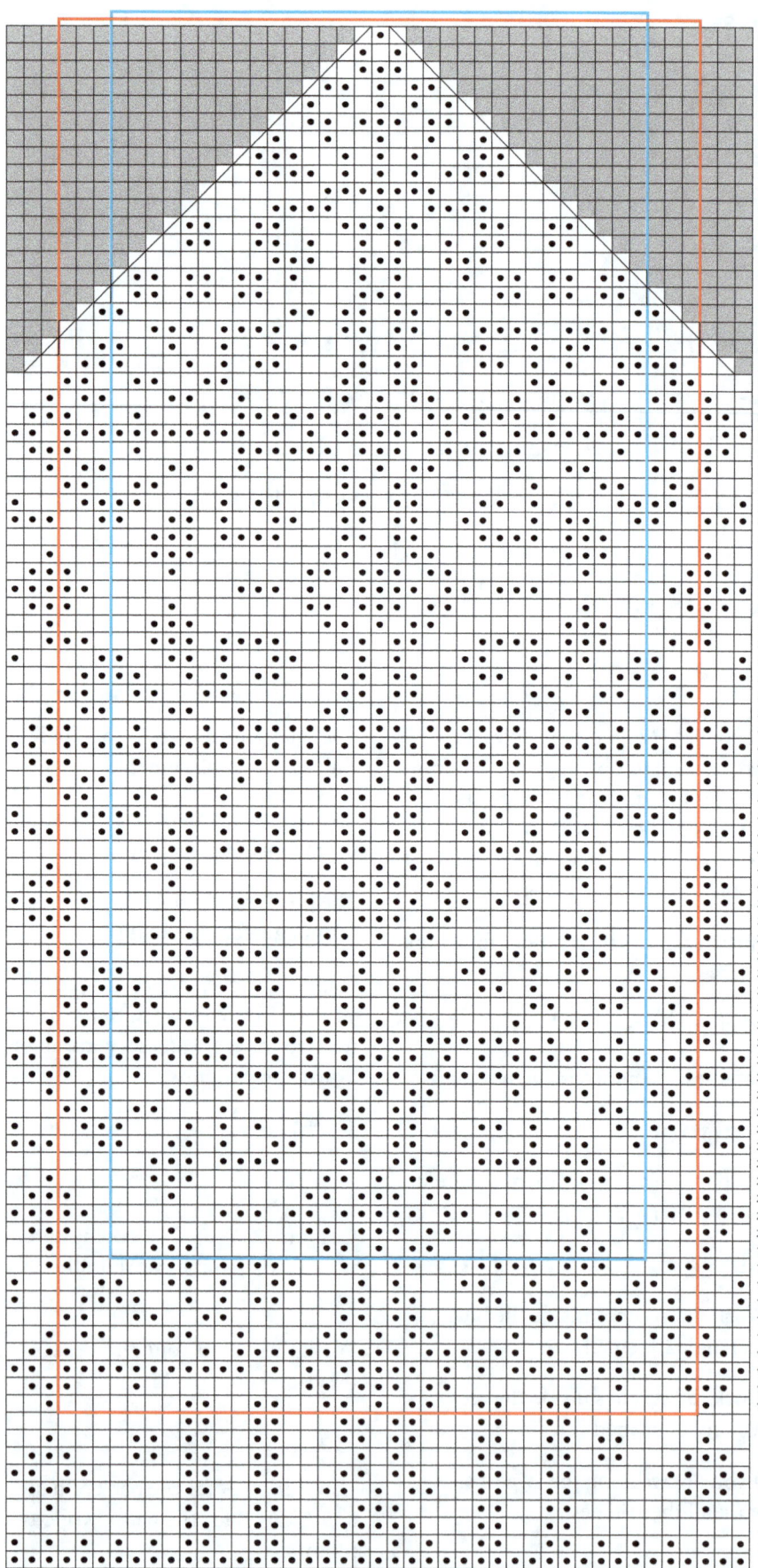

CHART A

Small: Work the stitches within both blue rectangles.

Medium: Work the stitches within both red rectangles.

Large: Work the whole chart.

Work as set, until rnd 27 (18, 9).

Thumb Gusset

All sizes

Left hand: Place a stitch marker either side of the color coded stitch for your size on the right hand side of your rectangle. Work the gusset chart between the stitch markers.

Right hand: Place a stitch marker either side of the color coded square for your size on the left hand side of your rectangle. Work the gusset chart between the stitch markers.

Work the hand charts as set until all increases have been completed.

Try on your mitten. Gusset length is as individual as you are. You may want to add some extra rounds before separating the thumb sts, you may also want to add some extra increases. It all depends on your hands. If you are adding extra rounds, just continue your thumb stitch pattern as set.

Once your thumb gusset is the length you want it, divide for the thumb as follows:

Work in pattern to first stitch marker, place the thumb sts on waste yarn or a stitch holder, cast on one st, work to the end of the round.

Continue to work the hand charts, as set until the last round is completed.

Break CC, and with MC, kitchener stitch the hand closed.

Thumb

Place your thumb sts back onto your needles, cast on 3 sts. - 22 (24, 26) sts.

Work the appropriate thumb chart. Break CC, with MC, kitchener stitch the thumb closed.

Stranded colorwork thumbs tend to be narrower than you'd expect. Try working your thumb with MC only, and use a duplicate stitch in CC for your stitch pattern after the thumb is completed.

Finishing

Weave in all ends, and wet block.

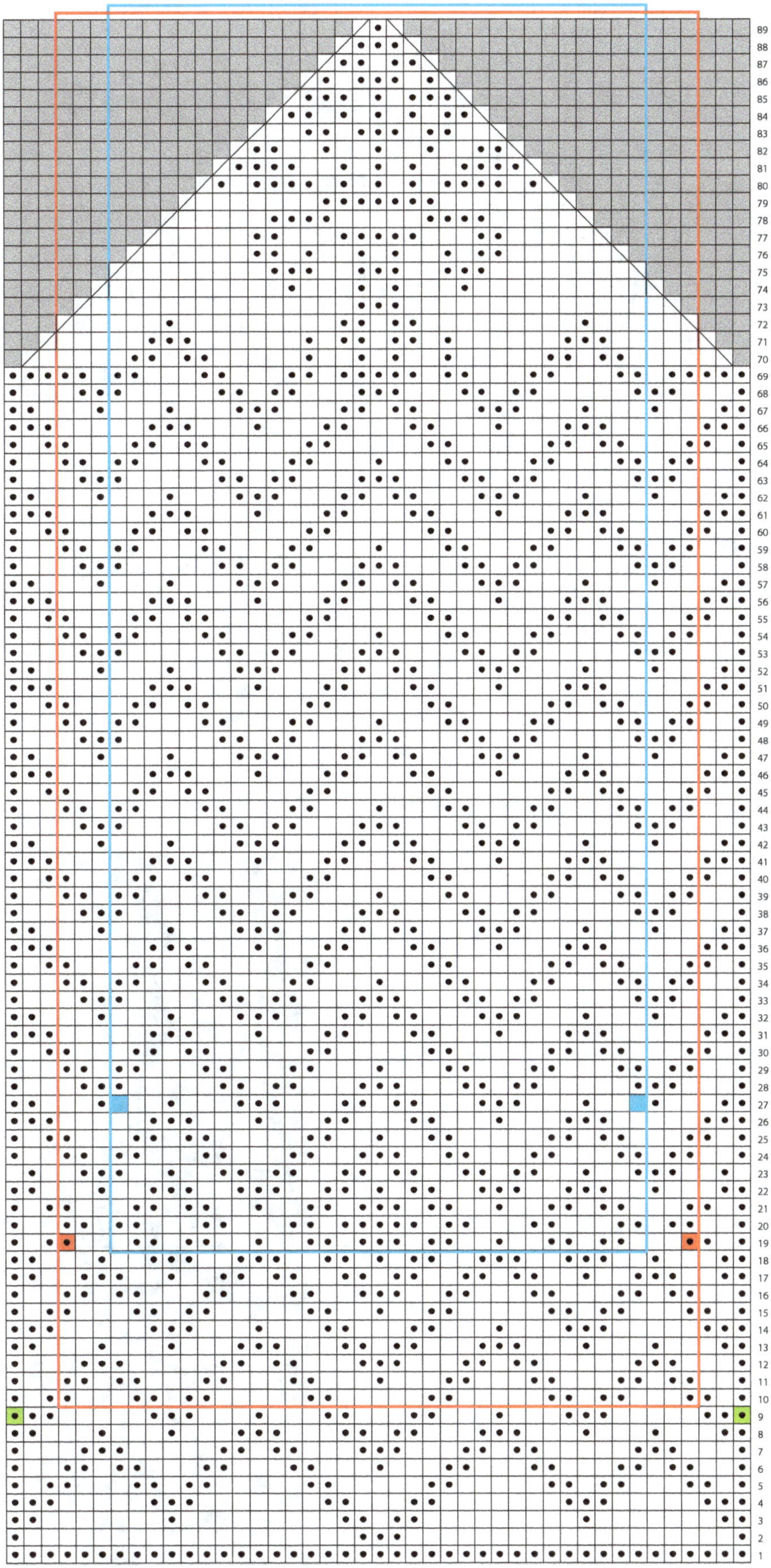

CHART B

Aurora Borealis Mittens | 48

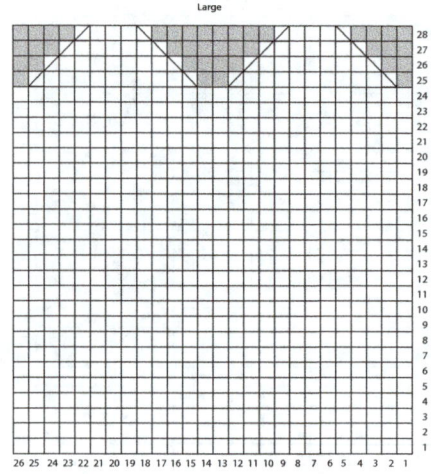
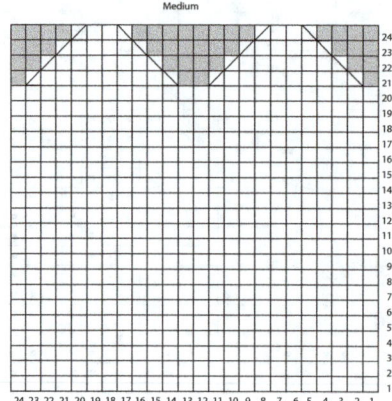
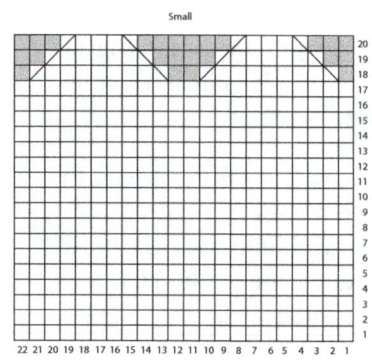

Thumb

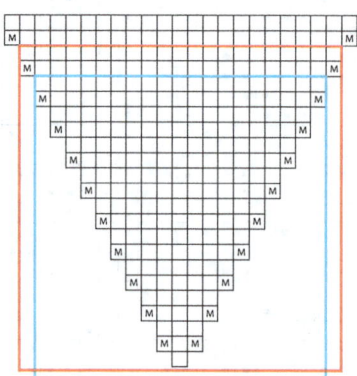

Aslaug

GRANDMA! As a recovering history grad student, I have a hard time taking some online genealogical records seriously, but if you care to believe them, I'm descended from Aslaug via her son Ivar the Boneless. (*A nickname we've called my cousin the meadmaker for years...seriously. And yes, I really do have a meadmaker cousin called Ivar. That's one fact I can easily prove!*) Ragnar Loðbrók proposed to Aslaug after a test of wits, which she passed handily. Sounds like she might have been a knitter, too.

Sizes

Women's S (M, L)

Shown in Large, with Cuff Option 2 added at the bottom and again, at round 18.

Finished Measurements

8 (9.25, 10.25)" / 20.32 (23.5, 26)cm circumference

6.8 (8.2, 9.5) " / 17.27 (20.82, 24.13) cm high without cuff

Materials

Knit Picks Palette yarn [100% Peruvian highland wool; 231 yds / 211m per 50g skein]; colors: Huckleberry Heather and Finnley Heather.

1 set US #1/2.25 mm needles, or size needed to obtain gauge. Choose needles for knitting in the round over a small circumference: dpns, two circulars, or one long circular for magic loop, as you prefer.

Waste yarn or stitch holder for thumb stitches

Stitch markers

Large-eyed, blunt sewing needle

Gauge

32 sts x 36 rnds = 4"/10cm square in stitch pattern.

Notes

Work the stitches inside the blue rectangle for small size

Work the stitches inside the red rectangle for medium size.

If you are working the largest size, work all the stitches.

The blue solid square is for small thumb gusset placement.

The red solid square is for medium thumb gusset placement.

The green solid square is for large thumb gusset placement.

Hands, however, are as unique as you are. Try on your mitten, you may need to move the gusset start up or down a few rounds.

Pattern

Cuff

Cast on 64 (74, 82) sts. Being careful not to twist, join to work in the round.

Work the cuff of your choice, as described on page 11.

Hand

Using Chart A for the back of hand, and Chart B for the palm, work as follows:

Small: Work the stitches within both blue rectangles.

Medium: Work the stitches within both red rectangles.

Aurora Borealis Mittens | 52

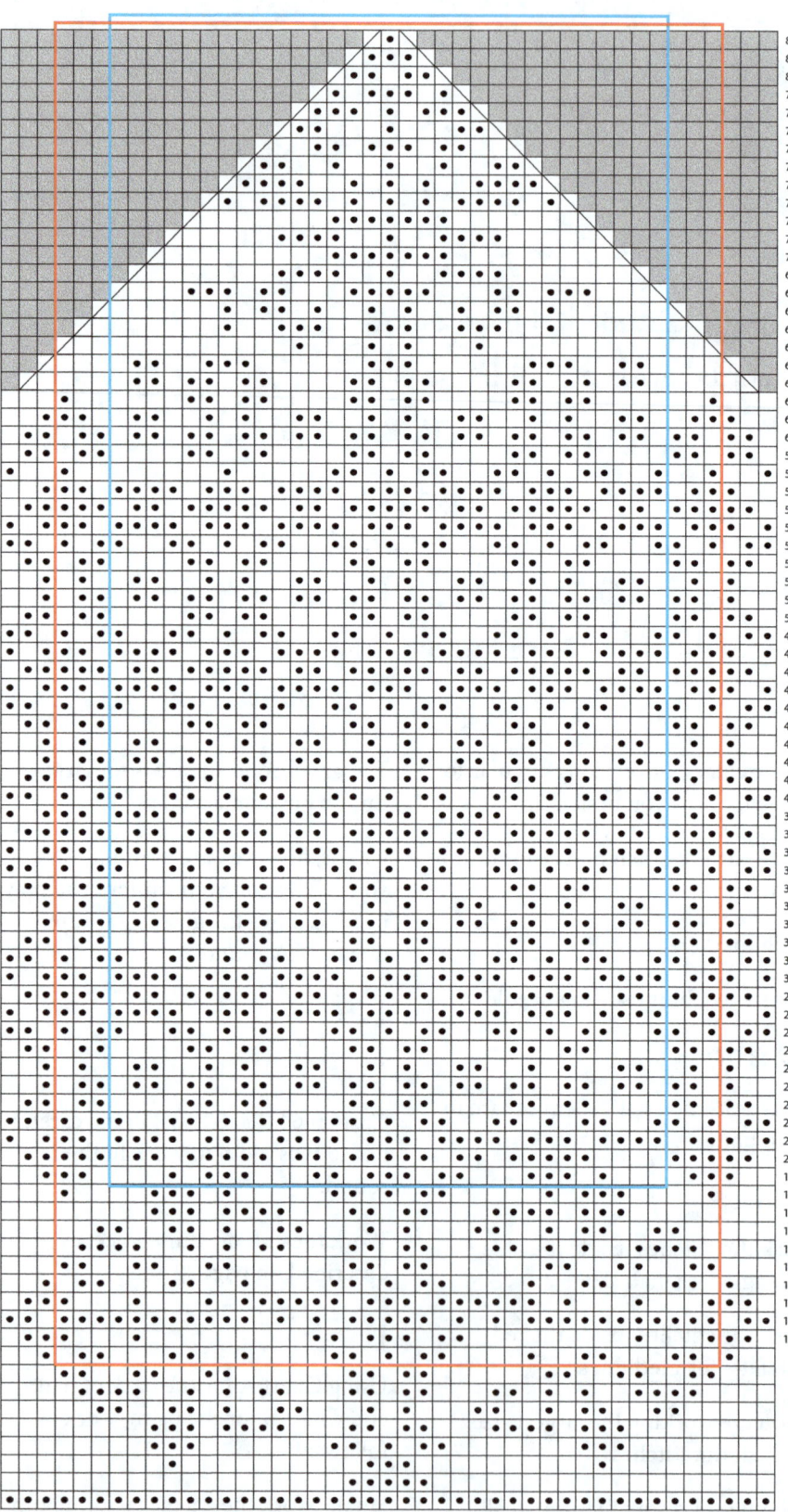

Chart A

Large: Work the whole chart.

Work as set, until rnd 27 (18, 9).

Thumb Gusset

All sizes

Left hand: Place a stitch marker either side of the color coded stitch for your size on the right hand side of your rectangle. Work the gusset chart between the stitch markers.

Right hand: Place a stitch marker either side of the color coded square for your size on the left hand side of your rectangle. Work the gusset chart between the stitch markers.

Work the hand charts as set until all increases have been completed.

Try on your mitten. Gusset length is as individual as you are. You may want to add some extra rounds before separating the thumb sts, you may also want to add some extra increases. It all depends on your hands. If you are adding extra rounds, just continue your thumb stitch pattern as set.

Once your thumb gusset is the length you want it, divide for the thumb as follows:

Work in pattern to first stitch marker, place the thumb sts on waste yarn or a stitch holder, cast on one st, work to the end of the round.

Continue to work the hand charts, as set until the last round is completed.

Break CC, and with MC, kitchener stitch the hand closed.

Aslaug | 53

Thumb

Place your thumb sts back onto your needles, cast on 3 sts. - 22 (24, 26) sts.

Work the appropriate thumb chart. Break CC, with MC, kitchener stitch the thumb closed.

Stranded colorwork thumbs tend to be narrower than you'd expect. Try working your thumb with MC only, and use a duplicate stitch in CC for your stitch pattern after the thumb is completed.

Finishing

Weave in all ends, and wet block.

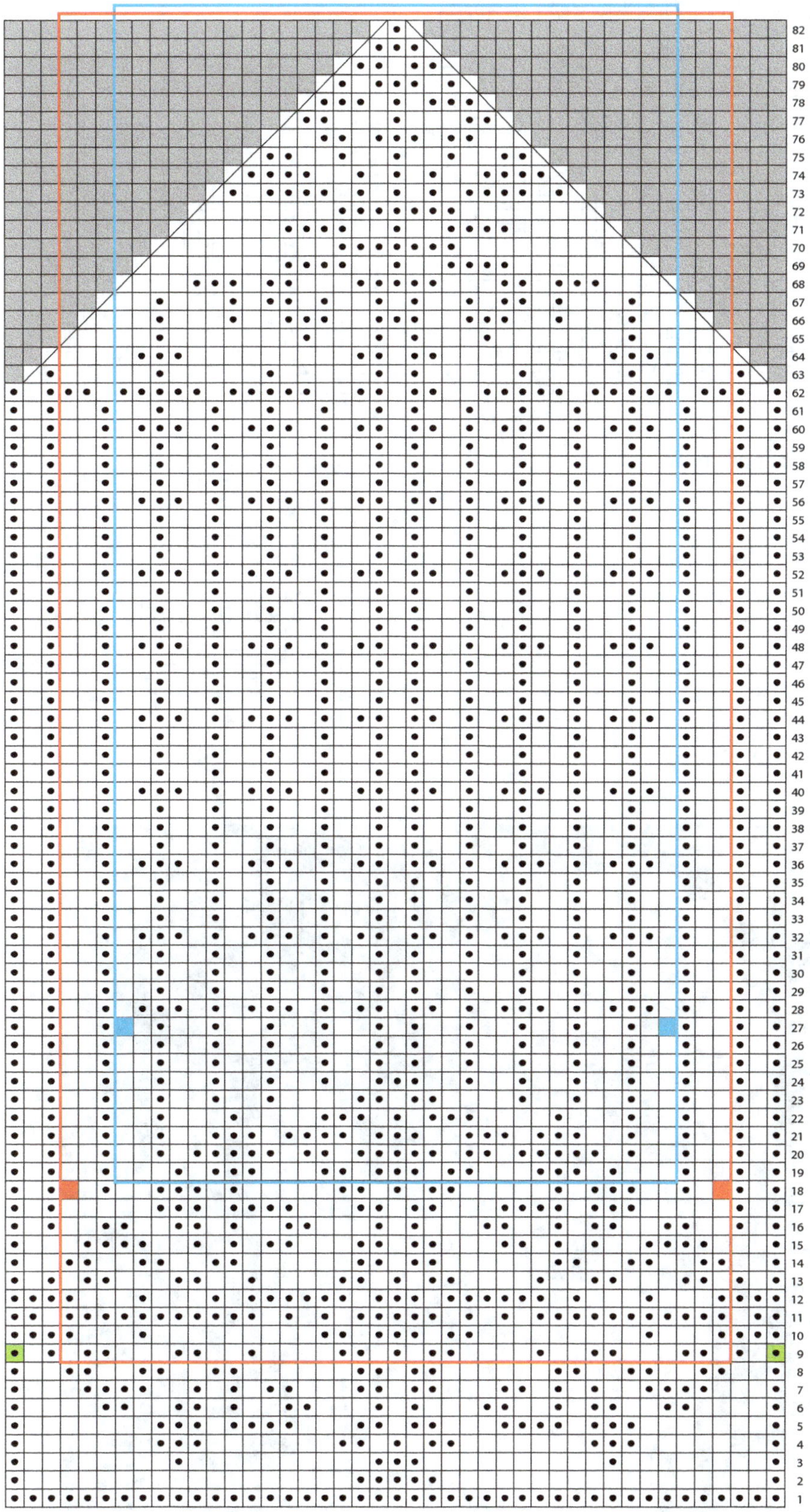

CHART B

Aurora Borealis Mittens | 54

Thumb

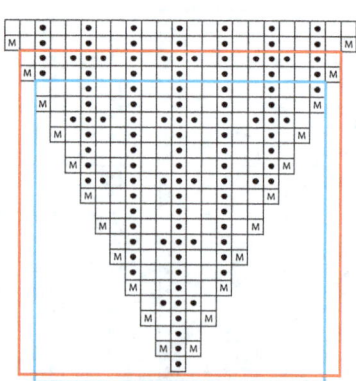

Eydis

Eydis is a name derived from the Norse word elements for "good fortune" and "goddess." A complex pattern that recalls both organic elements (leaves) and hardened lines like spears, I like to think of this mitten representing the Valkyries, mythic female figures who choose which warriors will leave the battlefield for Odin's feasting hall in Valhalla. They're your woolly shields against the cold.

Sizes

Women's S (M, L);

Shown in Large, with Cuff Option 5

Finished Measurements

8.25 (9.75, 11.25)" / 20.95 (24.75, 28.5)cm circumference

7.45 (8.5, 9.5)" / 18.9 (21.59, 24.13)cm high without cuff

Materials

Knit Picks Palette yarn [100% Peruvian highland wool; 231 yds / 211m per 50g skein]; colors: Celestial and Midnight Heather.

1 set US #1/2.25 mm needles, or size needed to obtain gauge. Choose needles for knitting in the round over a small circumference: dpns, two circulars, or one long circular for magic loop, as you prefer.

Waste yarn or stitch holder for thumb stitches

Stitch markers

Large-eyed, blunt sewing needle

Gauge

32 sts x 36 rnds = 4"/10cm square in stitch pattern.

Notes

Work the stitches inside the blue rectangle for small size

Work the stitches inside the red rectangle for medium size.

If you are working the largest size, work all the stitches.

The blue solid square is for small thumb gusset placement.

The red solid square is for medium thumb gusset placement.

The green solid square is for large thumb gusset placement.

Hands, however, are as unique as you are. Try on your mitten, you may need to move the gusset start up or down a few rounds.

Pattern

Cuff

Cast on 66 (78, 90) sts. Being careful not to twist, join to work in the round.

Work the cuff of your choice, as described on page 11.

Hand

Using chart A for the back of hand, and Chart B for the palm, work as follows:

Small: Work the stitches within both blue rectangles.

Medium: Work the stitches within both red rectangles.

Large: Work the whole chart.

Work as set, until rnd 27 (18, 9).

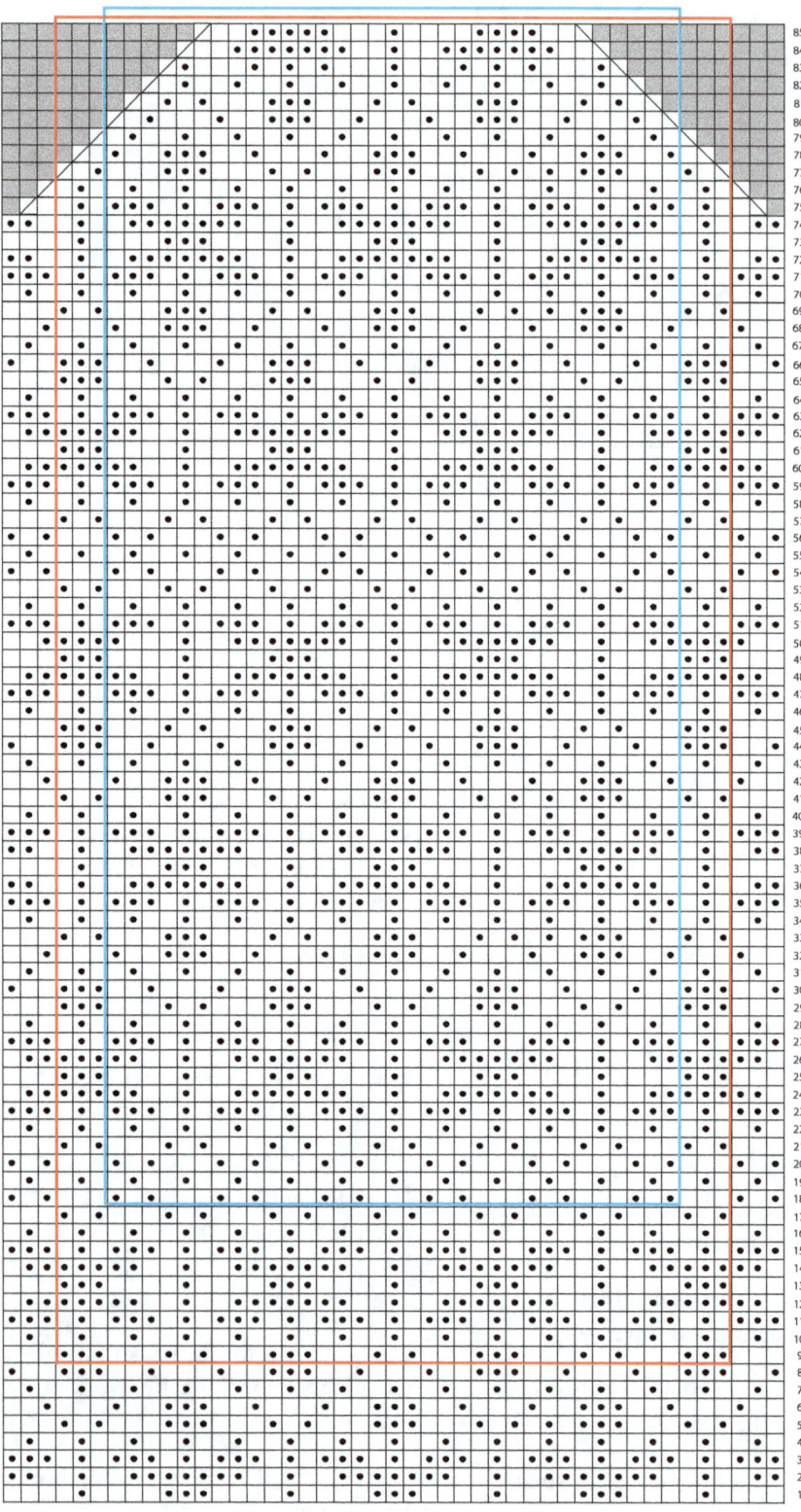

CHART A

Thumb Gusset

All sizes

Left hand: Place a stitch marker either side of the color coded stitch for your size on the right hand side of your rectangle. Work the gusset chart between the stitch markers.

Right hand: Place a stitch marker either side of the color coded square for your size on the left hand side of your rectangle. Work the gusset chart between the stitch markers.

Work the hand charts as set until all increases have been completed.

Try on your mitten. Gusset length is as individual as you are. You may want to add some extra rounds before separating the thumb sts, you may also want to add some extra increases. It all depends on your hands. If you are adding extra rounds, just continue your thumb stitch pattern as set.

Once your thumb gusset is the length you want it, divide for the thumb as follows:

Work in pattern to first stitch marker, place the thumb sts on waste yarn or a stitch holder, cast on one st, work to the end of the round.

Continue to work the hand charts, as set until the last round is completed.

Break CC, and with MC, kitchener stitch the hand closed.

Thumb

Place your thumb sts back onto your needles, cast on 3 sts. - 22 (24, 26) sts.

Work the appropriate thumb chart. Break CC, with MC, kitchener stitch the thumb closed.

Stranded colorwork thumbs tend to be narrower than you'd expect. Try working your thumb with MC only, and use a duplicate stitch in CC for your stitch pattern after the thumb is completed.

Finishing

Weave in all ends, and wet block.

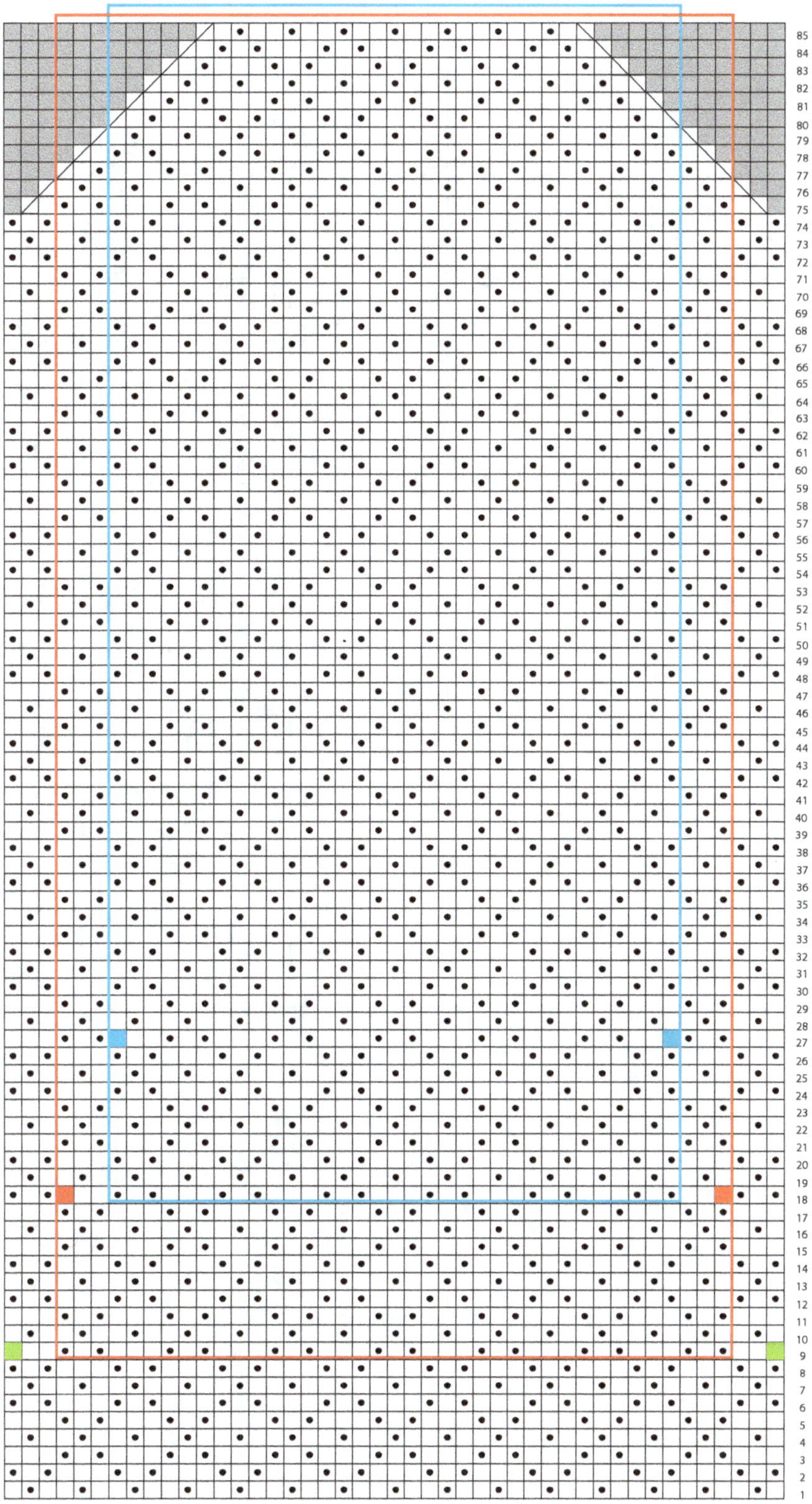

CHART B

Aurora Borealis Mittens | 60

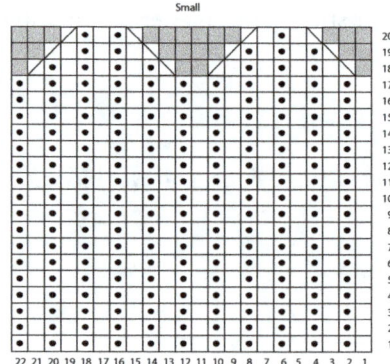

Thumb

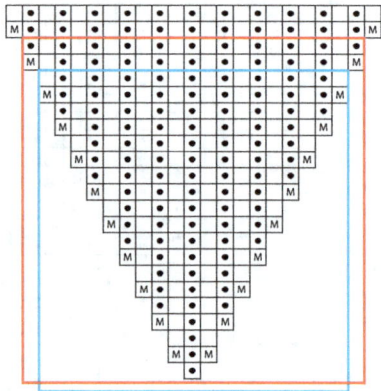

Astrid (Old Norse Æstriðr) was a powerful, rich 11th-century woman whose history was recorded on a series of runestones found near Uppsala, Sweden. Her husband fought in Jerusalem and died in the Byzantine Empire—no doubt having sent back some exotic riches along the way, as did so many through the trade routes. The elite Varangian Guard of the Byzantine Empire was composed predominantly of Norse warriors. Princess and chronicler Anna Komnene referred to them as "axe-bearing barbarians from Thule" in her writings, including the *Alexiad*.

Sizes

Women's S (M, L)

Main picture shown in Large, with Cuff Option 5

Secondary picture shown in Large, with Cuff Option 4

Finished Measurements

8.25 (9.75, 11.25)" / 20.95 (24.75, 28.5)cm circumference

7.45 (8.5, 9.5)" / 18.9 (21.59, 24.13)cm high without cuff

Materials

Knit Picks Palette yarn [100% Peruvian highland wool; 231 yds / 211m per 50g skein]; colors: Raspberry Heather and Finnley Heather.

Baah Yarn La Jolla yarn [100% superwash merino wool,; 400 yds / 365m per 100g skein]; colors: London Blue and Grey Onyx;

1 set US #1/2.25 mm needles, or size needed to obtain gauge. Choose needles for knitting in the round over a small circumference: dpns, two circulars, or one long circular for magic loop, as you prefer.

Waste yarn or stitch holder for thumb stitches

Stitch markers

Large-eyed, blunt sewing needle

Gauge

32 sts x 36 rnds = 4"/10cm square in stitch pattern.

Notes

Work the stitches inside the blue rectangle for small size

Work the stitches inside the red rectangle for medium size.

If you are working the largest size, work all the stitches.

The blue solid square is for small thumb gusset placement.

The red solid square is for medium thumb gusset placement.

The green solid square is for large thumb gusset placement.

Hands, however, are as unique as you are. Try on your mitten, you may need to move the gusset start up or down a few rounds.

Pattern

Cuff

Cast on 66 (78, 90) sts. Being careful not to twist, join to work in the round.

Work the cuff of your choice, as described on page 11.

Aurora Borealis Mittens | 64

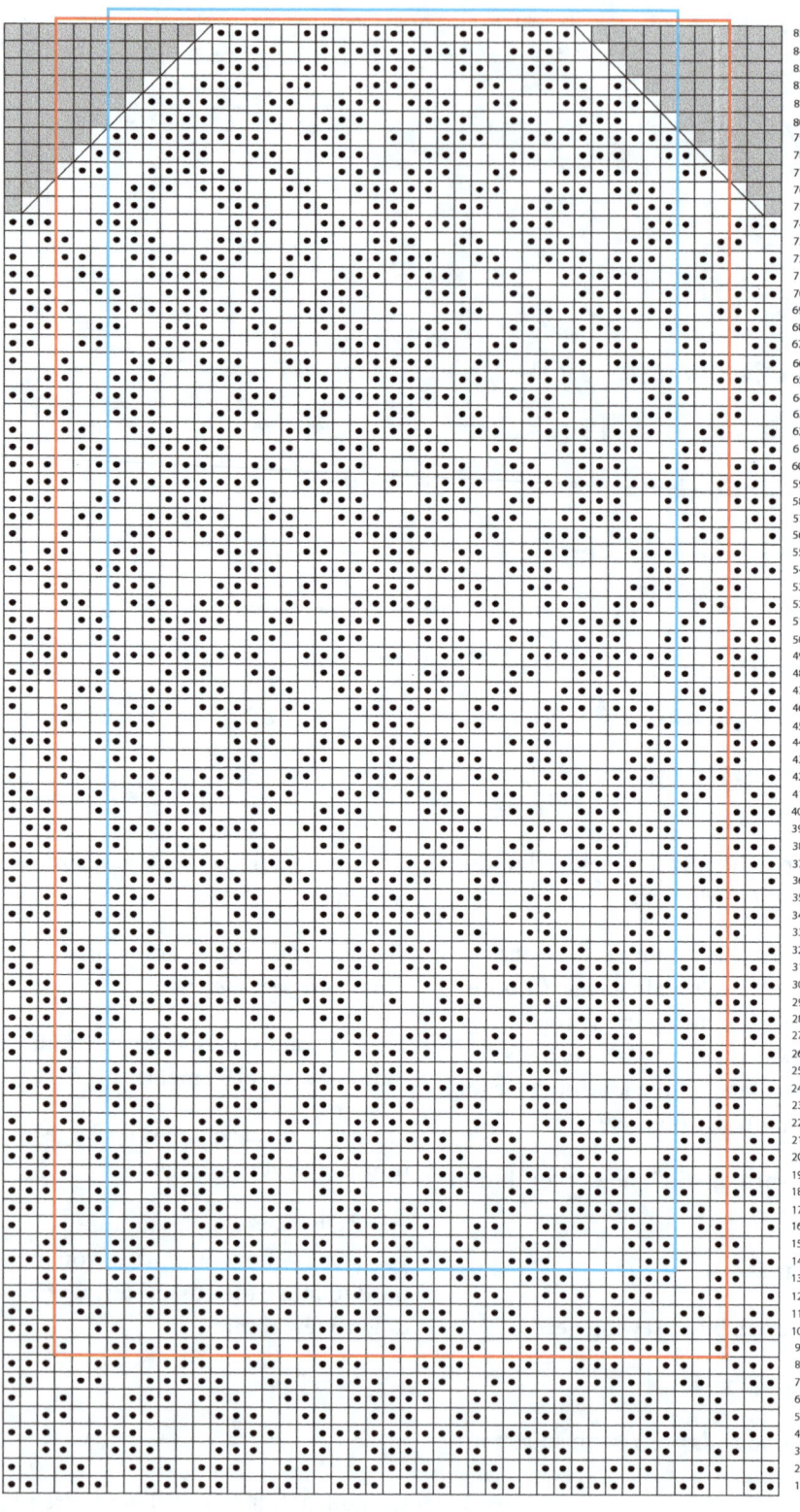

CHART A

Hand

Using chart A for the back of hand, and Chart B for the palm, work as follows:

Small: Work the stitches within both blue rectangles.

Medium: Work the stitches within both red rectangles.

Large: Work the whole chart.

Work as set, until rnd 27 (18, 9).

Thumb Gusset

All sizes

Left hand: Place a stitch marker either side of the color coded stitch for your size on the right hand side of your rectangle. Work the gusset chart between the stitch markers.

Right hand: Place a stitch marker either side of the color coded square for your size on the left hand side of your rectangle. Work the gusset chart between the stitch markers.

Work the hand charts as set until all increases have been completed.

Try on your mitten. Gusset length is as individual as you are. You may want to add some extra rounds before separating the thumb sts, you may also want to add some extra increases. It all depends on your hands. If you are adding extra rounds, just continue your thumb stitch pattern as set.

Once your thumb gusset is the length you want it, divide for the thumb as follows:

Work in pattern to first stitch marker, place the thumb sts on waste yarn or a stitch holder, cast on one st, work to the end of the round.

Astrid | 65

Continue to work the hand charts, as set until the last round is completed.

Break CC, and with MC, kitchener stitch the hand closed.

Thumb

Place your thumb sts back onto your needles, cast on 3 sts. - 22 (24, 26) sts.

Work the appropriate thumb chart. Break CC, with MC, kitchener stitch the thumb closed.

Stranded colorwork thumbs tend to be narrower than you'd expect. Try working your thumb with MC only, and use a duplicate stitch in CC for your stitch pattern after the thumb is completed.

Finishing

Weave in all ends, and wet block.

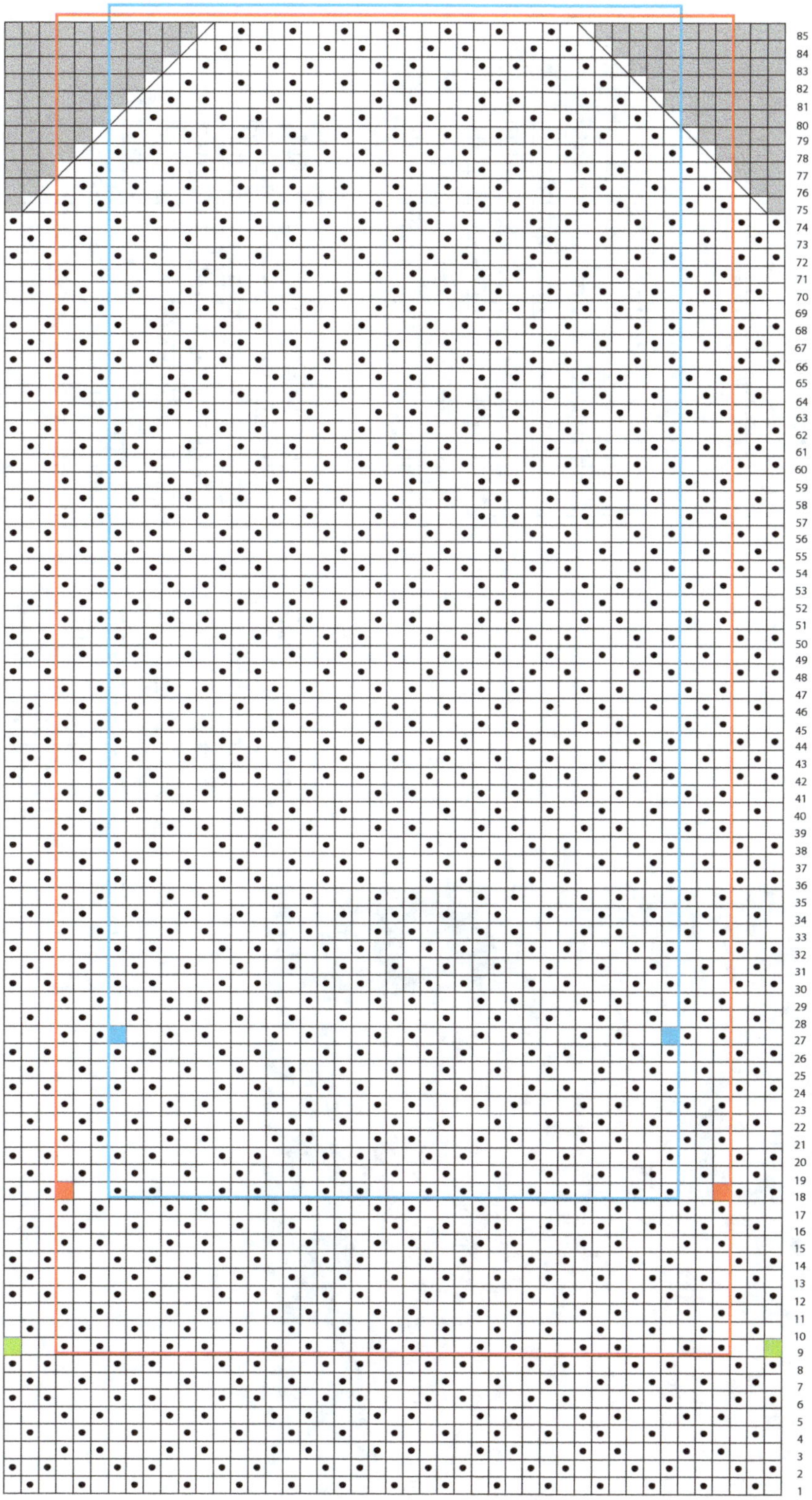

CHART B

Aurora Borealis Mittens | 66

Thumb

Iðunn's Garden

In Norse myth, Iðunn is the goddess associated with apples and youth. Loki, in typical Loki-is-a-jerk fashion, lured her out of Asgard with the promise of interesting apples, with the unexpected side effect of causing all the gods to grow grey and old. I like to think that Iðunn wised up after that and kept her garden hidden behind a gate, as seen in the design here, to prevent further mischief.

Sizes

Women's M, L

Main picture shown in Large, with Cuff Option 5

Secondary picture shown in Large with plain bindoff.

Measurements

Finished Measurements

9.5 (10.5)" / 24.13 (26.67)cm circumference

9.4 (10.5)" / 23.87 (26.67)cm high without cuff

Materials

Fiber Optic Foot Notes Sock yarn [80% superwash merino wool, 20% nylon; 435 yds / 398m per 113g skein]; colors: Raspberry and gradient kit Dusty Plum to Olive Foot Notes Paintbox

1 set US #1/2.25 mm needles, or size needed to obtain gauge. Choose needles for knitting in the round over a small circumference: dpns, two circulars, or one long circular for magic loop, as you prefer.

Waste yarn or stitch holder for thumb stitches

Stitch markers

Large-eyed, blunt sewing needle

Gauge

32 sts x 36 rnds = 4"/10cm square in stitch pattern.

Notes

Work the stitches inside the red rectangle for medium size.

If you are working the largest size, work all the stitches.

The red solid square is for medium thumb gusset placement.

The green solid square is for large thumb gusset placement.

Hands, however, are as unique as you are. Try on your mitten, you may need to move the gusset start up or down a few rounds.

Pattern

Cuff

Cast on 76 (84) sts. Being careful not to twist, join to work in the round.

Work the cuff of your choice, as described on page 11.

Hand

Using Chart A for the back of hand, and Chart B for the palm, work as follows:

Medium: Work the stitches within both red rectangles.

Large: Work the whole chart.

Work as set, until rnd 32 (24).

Aurora Borealis Mittens | 70

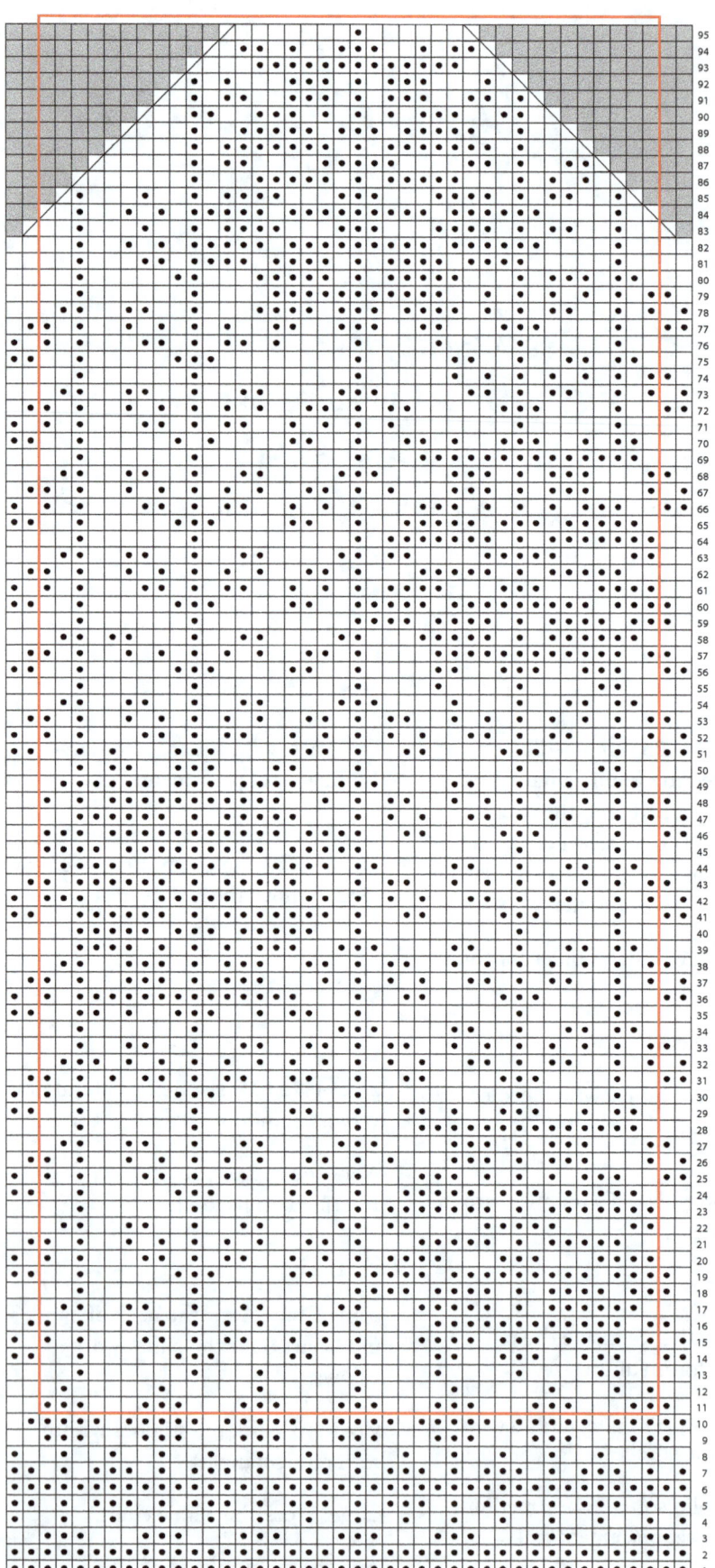

CHART A LEFT MITTEN

Thumb Gusset

All sizes

Left hand: Place a stitch marker either side of the color coded stitch for your size on the right hand side of your rectangle. Work the gusset chart between the stitch markers.

Right hand: Place a stitch marker either side of the color coded square for your size on the left hand side of your rectangle. Work the gusset chart between the stitch markers.

Work the hand charts as set until all increases have been completed.

Try on your mitten. Gusset length is as individual as you are. You may want to add some extra rounds before separating the thumb sts, you may also want to add some extra increases. It all depends on your hands. If you are adding extra rounds, just continue your thumb stitch pattern as set.

Once your thumb gusset is the length you want it, divide for the thumb as follows:

Work in pattern to first stitch marker, place the thumb sts on waste yarn or a stitch holder, cast on one st, work to the end of the round.

Continue to work the hand charts, as set until the last round is completed.

Break CC, and with MC, kitchener stitch the hand closed.

Continue to work the hand charts, as set until the last round is completed.

Break CC, and with MC, kitchener stitch the hand closed.

Idunn's Garden | 71

Thumb

Place your thumb sts back onto your needles, cast on 3 sts. - 24 (26) sts.

Work the appropriate thumb chart. Break CC, with MC, kitchener stitch the thumb closed.

Stranded colorwork thumbs tend to be narrower than you'd expect. Try working your thumb with MC only, and use a duplicate stitch in CC for your stitch pattern after the thumb is completed.

Finishing

Weave in all ends, and wet block.

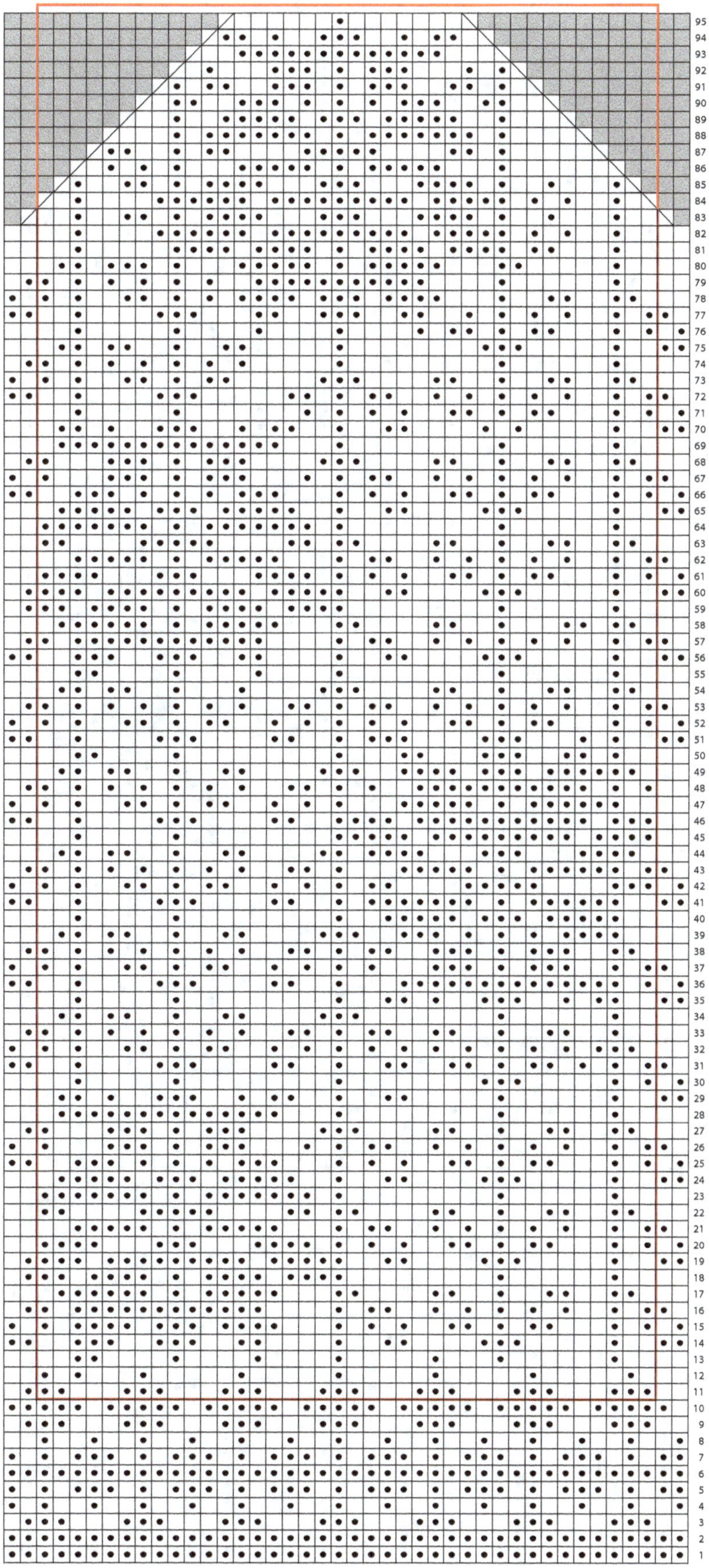

CHART A RIGHT MITTEN

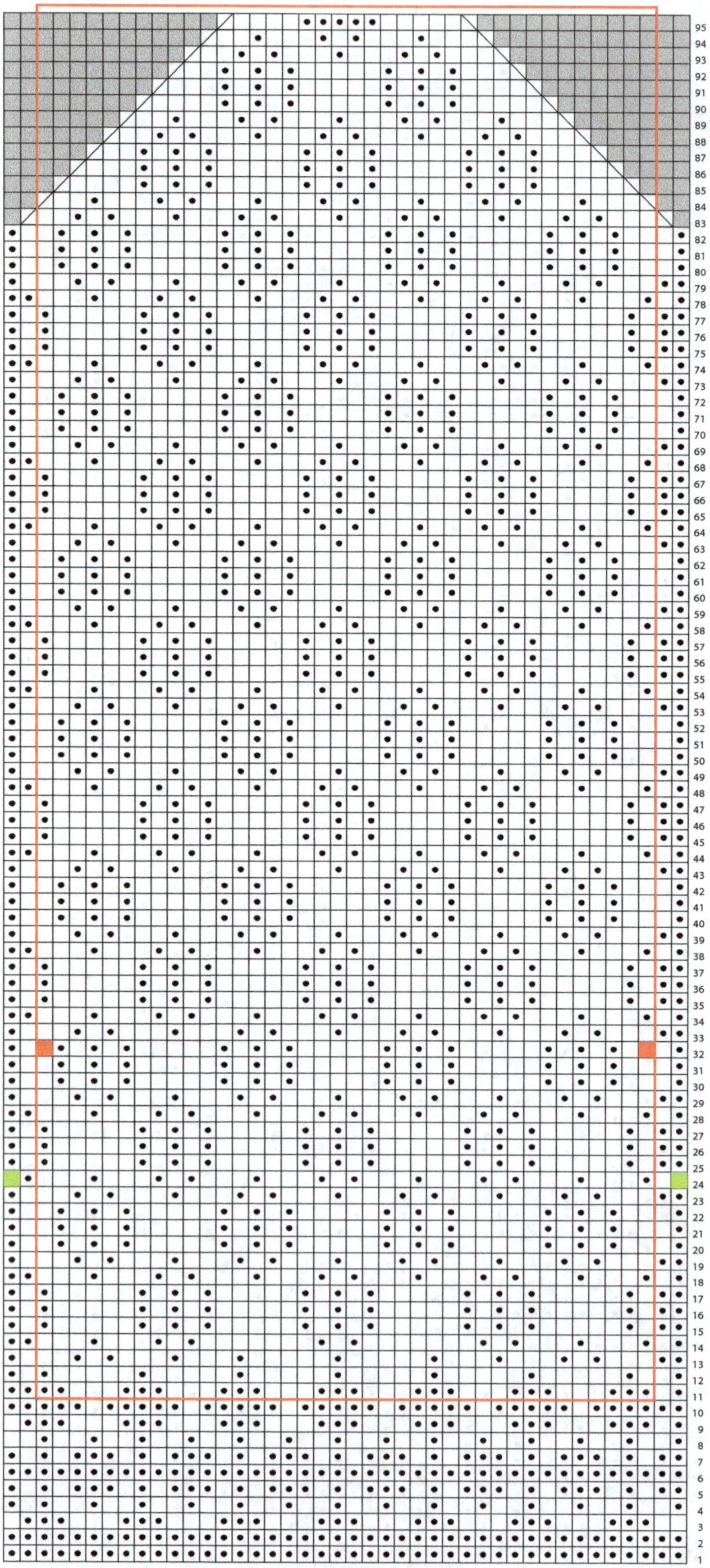

Aurora Borealis Mittens | 72

CHART B

Idunn's Garden | 73

Large

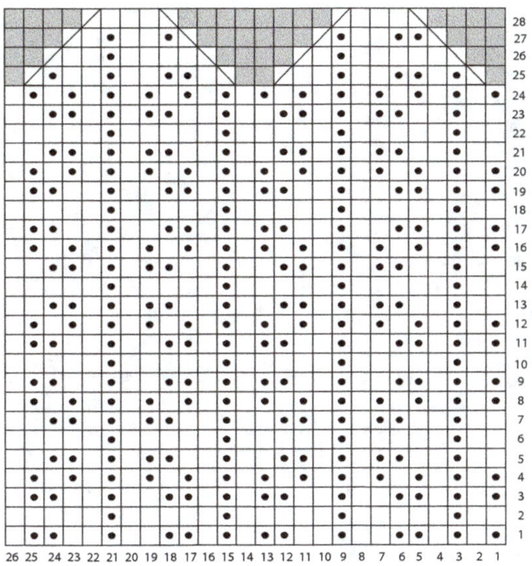

Medium

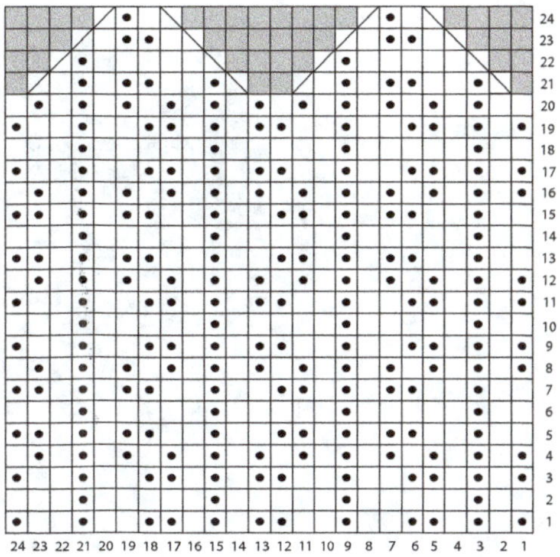

Thumb

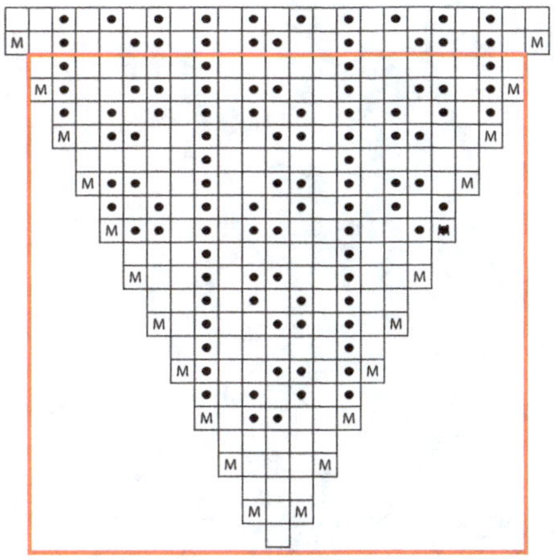

Freydis

Freydis, bad girl of vinland exploration! Daughter of Erik the Red, general badass and—if you believe the hype—greedy murderer and betrayer of business partners. While under attack, the men from her settlement ran off into the woods. Freydis, who was pregnant at the time, grabbed a sword off a dead guy, dropped her top and sliced open her own breast, both freaking out and scaring off their attackers. (This after she'd said: "Let me but have a weapon, I think I could fight better than any of you.") Me, I think they gave her a bad rap afterwards because she embarassed her male companions. Yup. Badass.

Sizes

Women's S (M, L)

Both shown in Large with Cuff Option 5

Finished Measurements

8 (9.5, 11)" / 20.32 (24.13, 27.94)cm circumference

9.4 (8.4, 9.4)" / 18.8 (21.34, 23.88)cm high without cuff

Materials

Purple and grey pair: Neighborhood Fiber Co. Studio Sock yarn [100% superwash merino wool; 400 yds / 366m per 113g skein]; colors: Truxton and Thomas Circle

Coral and silver pair: Knit Picks Palette yarn [100% Peruvian highland wool; 231 yds / 211m per 50g skein]; colors: Conch and Silver

1 set US #1/2.25 mm needles, or size needed to obtain gauge. Choose needles for knitting in the round over a small circumference: dpns, two circulars, or one long circular for magic loop, as you prefer.

Waste yarn or stitch holder for thumb stitches

Stitch markers

Large-eyed, blunt sewing needle

Gauge

32 sts x 36 rnds = 4"/10cm square in stitch pattern.

Notes

Work the stitches inside the blue rectangle for small size.

Work the stitches inside the red rectangle for medium size.

If you are working the largest size, work all the stitches.

The blue solid square is for small thumb gusset placement.

The red solid square is for medium thumb gusset placement.

The green solid square is for large thumb gusset placement.

Hands, however, are as unique as you are. Try on your mitten, you may need to move the gusset start up or down a few rounds.

Pattern

Cuff

Cast on 64 (76, 88) sts. Being careful not to twist, join to work in the round.

Aurora Borealis Mittens | 78

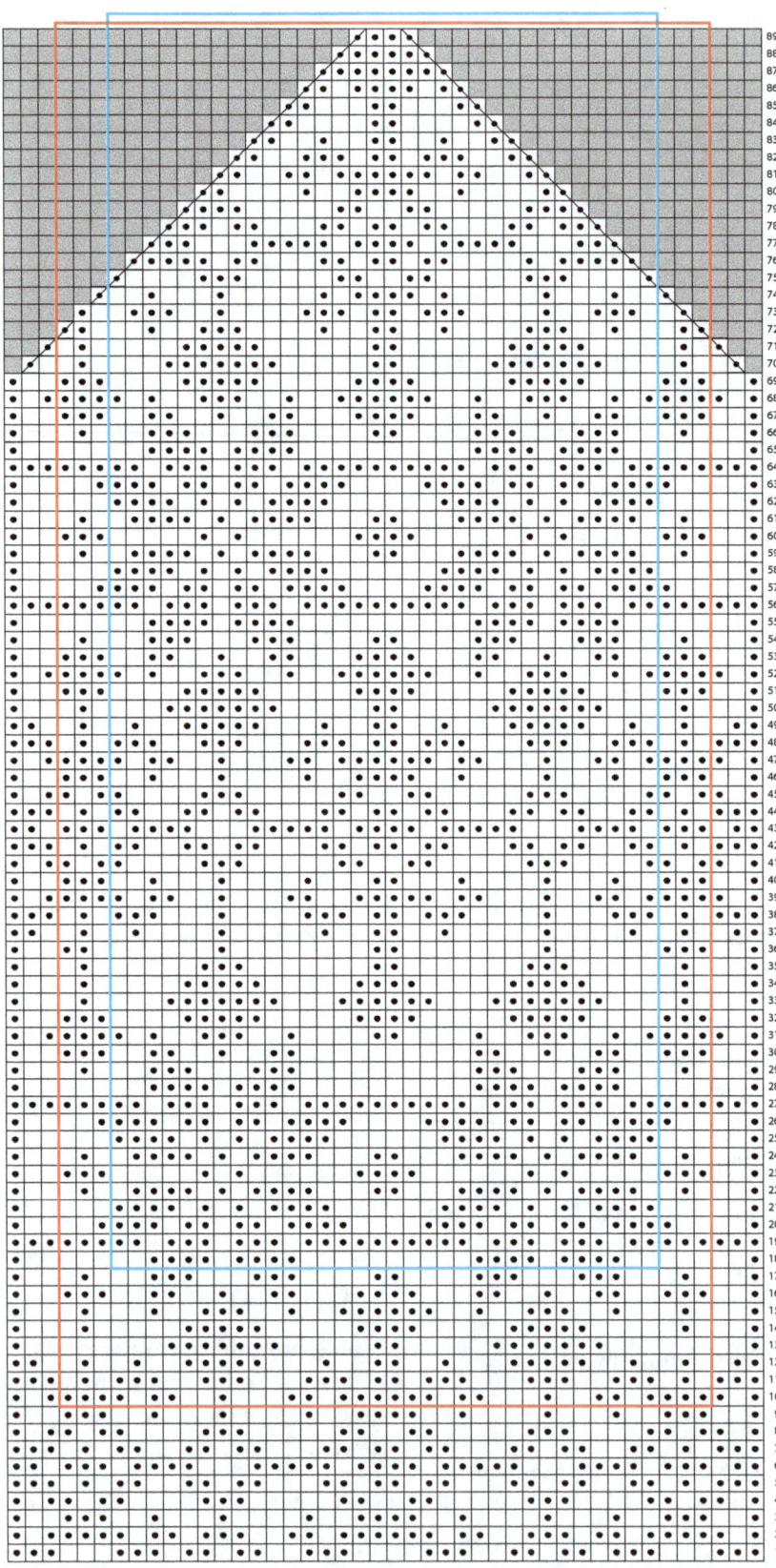

Chart A

Work the cuff of your choice, as described on page 11.

Hand

Using chart A for the back of hand, and Chart B for the palm, work as follows:

Small: Work the stitches within both blue rectangles.

Medium: Work the stitches within both red rectangles.

Large: Work the whole chart.

Work as set, until rnd 27 (18, 9).

Thumb Gusset

All sizes

Left hand: Place a stitch marker either side of the color coded stitch for your size on the right hand side of your rectangle. Work the gusset chart between the stitch markers.

Right hand: Place a stitch marker either side of the color coded square for your size on the left hand side of your rectangle. Work the gusset chart between the stitch markers.

Work the hand charts as set until all increases have been completed.

Try on your mitten. Gusset length is as individual as you are. You may want to add some extra rounds before separating the thumb sts, you may also want to add some extra increases. It all depends on your hands. If you are adding extra rounds, just continue your thumb stitch pattern as set.

Once your thumb gusset is the length you want it, divide for the thumb as follows:

Work in pattern to first stitch marker, place the thumb sts on waste yarn or a stitch holder, cast on one st, work to the end of the round.

Freydis | 79

Continue to work the hand charts, as set until the last round is completed.

Break CC, and with MC, kitchener stitch the hand closed.

Thumb

Place your thumb sts back onto your needles, cast on 3 sts. - 22 (24, 26) sts.

Work the appropriate thumb chart. Break CC, with MC, kitchener stitch the thumb closed.

Stranded colorwork thumbs tend to be narrower than you'd expect. Try working your thumb with MC only, and use a duplicate stitch in CC for your stitch pattern after the thumb is completed.

Finishing

Weave in all ends, and wet block.

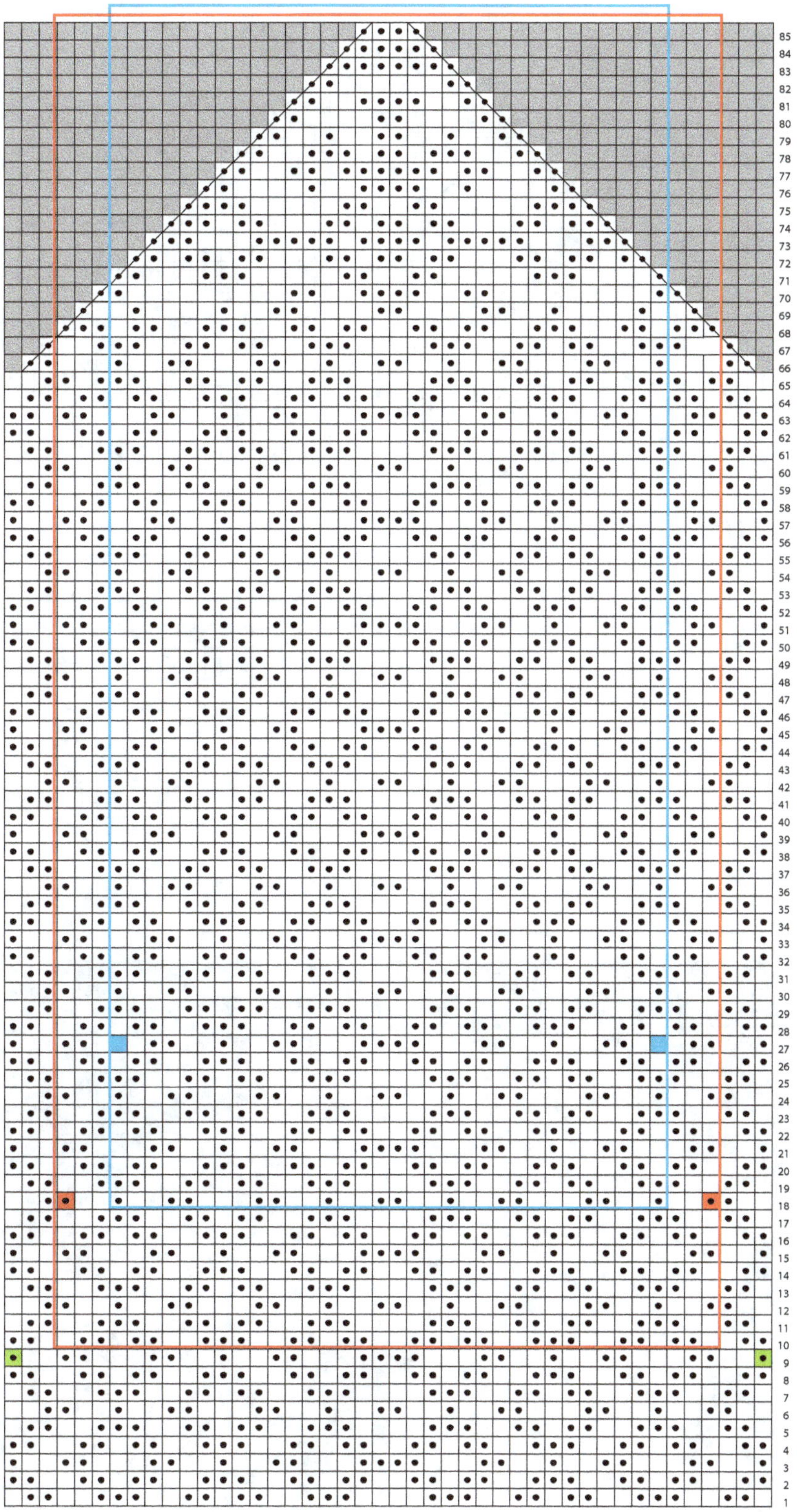

CHART B

Aurora Borealis Mittens | 80

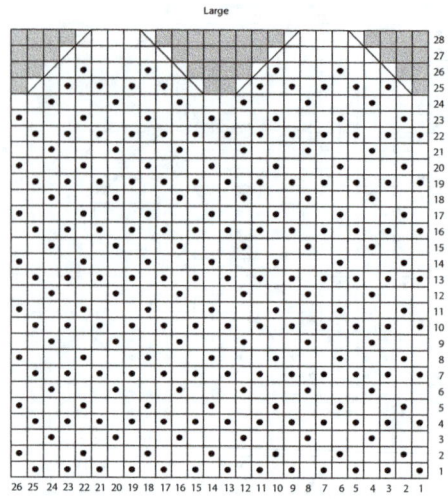

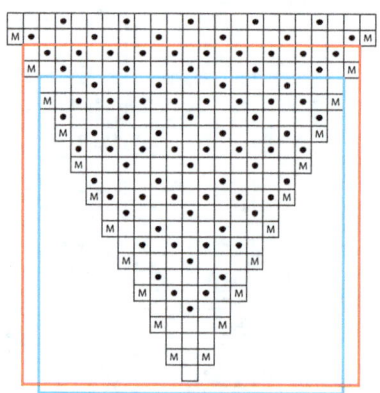

Thumb

Sindri

Both the name of a dwarf (and dwarves are all about the gold in Norse myth) and the name of a golden hall where the righteous will live after Ragnarok, Sindri was designed with a variation on a traditional Nordic star motif, but featuring the shining golden color of Cephalopod's Red Eft colorway, with deep Blue Lobster representing the underground homes where the dwarves mine their gold. It will, however, look spectacular in any colors you choose.

Sizes

Women's S (M, L)

Shown in Large, with Cuff Options 5 and 2

Finished Measurements

8 (9.5, 11)" / 20.32 (24.13, 27.94)cm circumference

8.75 (10, 11)" / 22.23 (25.4, 27.94)cm high without cuff

Materials

Cephalopod Yarns Skinny Bugga yarn [80% superwash merino wool, 10% nylon, 10% cashmere; 424 yds / 398m per 113g skein]; colors: Red Eft and Blue Lobster

1 set US #1/2.25 mm needles, or size needed to obtain gauge. Choose needles for knitting in the round over a small circumference: dpns, two circulars, or one long circular for magic loop, as you prefer.

Waste yarn or stitch holder for thumb stitches

Stitch markers

Large-eyed, blunt sewing needle

Gauge

32 sts x 36 rnds = 4"/10cm square in stitch pattern.

Notes

Work the stitches inside the blue rectangle for small size.

Work the stitches inside the red rectangle for medium size.

If you are working the largest size, work all the stitches.

The blue solid square is for small thumb gusset placement.

The red solid square is for medium thumb gusset placement.

The green solid square is for large thumb gusset placement.

Hands, however, are as unique as you are. Try on your mitten, you may need to move the gusset start up or down a few rounds.

Pattern

Cuff

Cast on 64 (76, 88) sts. Being careful not to twist, join to work in the round.

Work the cuff of your choice, as described on page 11.

Hand

Using chart A for the back of hand, and Chart B for the palm, work as follows:

Small: Work the stitches within both blue rectangles.

Medium: Work the stitches within both red rectangles.

Large: Work the whole chart.

Work as set, until rnd 27 (18, 9).

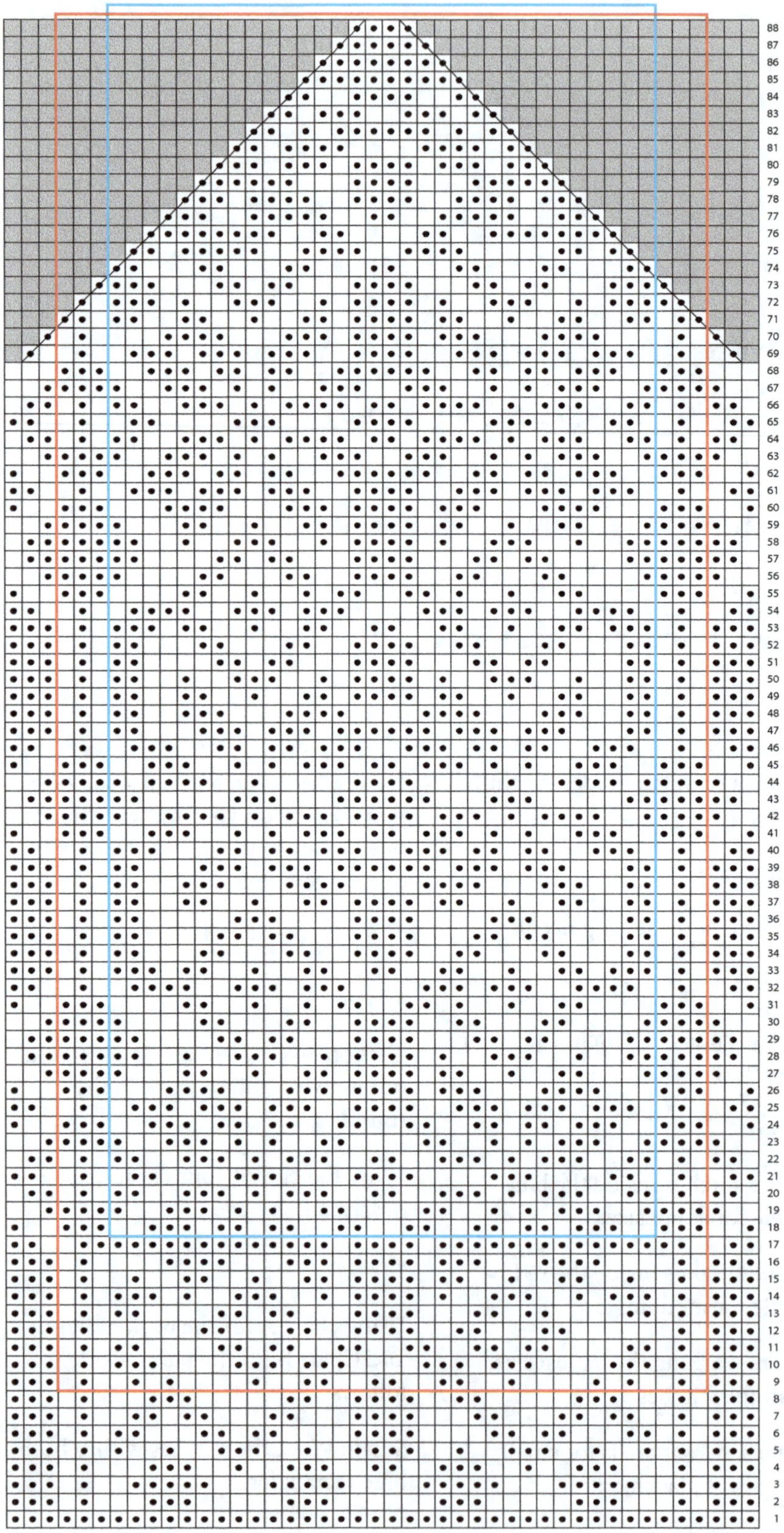

Aurora Borealis Mittens | 84

Thumb Gusset

All sizes

Left hand: Place a stitch marker either side of the color coded stitch for your size on the right hand side of your rectangle. Work the gusset chart between the stitch markers.

Right hand: Place a stitch marker either side of the color coded square for your size on the left hand side of your rectangle. Work the gusset chart between the stitch markers.

Work the hand charts as set until all increases have been completed.

Try on your mitten. Gusset length is as individual as you are. You may want to add some extra rounds before separating the thumb sts, you may also want to add some extra increases. It all depends on your hands. If you are adding extra rounds, just continue your thumb stitch pattern as set.

Once your thumb gusset is the length you want it, divide for the thumb as follows:

Work in pattern to first stitch marker, place the thumb sts on waste yarn or a stitch holder, cast on one st, work to the end of the round.

Continue to work the hand charts, as set until the last round is completed.

Break CC, and with MC, kitchener stitch the hand closed.

Thumb

Place your thumb sts back onto your needles, cast on 3 sts. - 22 (24, 26) sts.

Work the appropriate thumb chart. Break CC, with MC, kitchener stitch the thumb closed.

CHART A

Stranded colorwork thumbs tend to be narrower than you'd expect. Try working your thumb with MC only, and use a duplicate stitch in CC for your stitch pattern after the thumb is completed.

Finishing

Weave in all ends, and wet block.

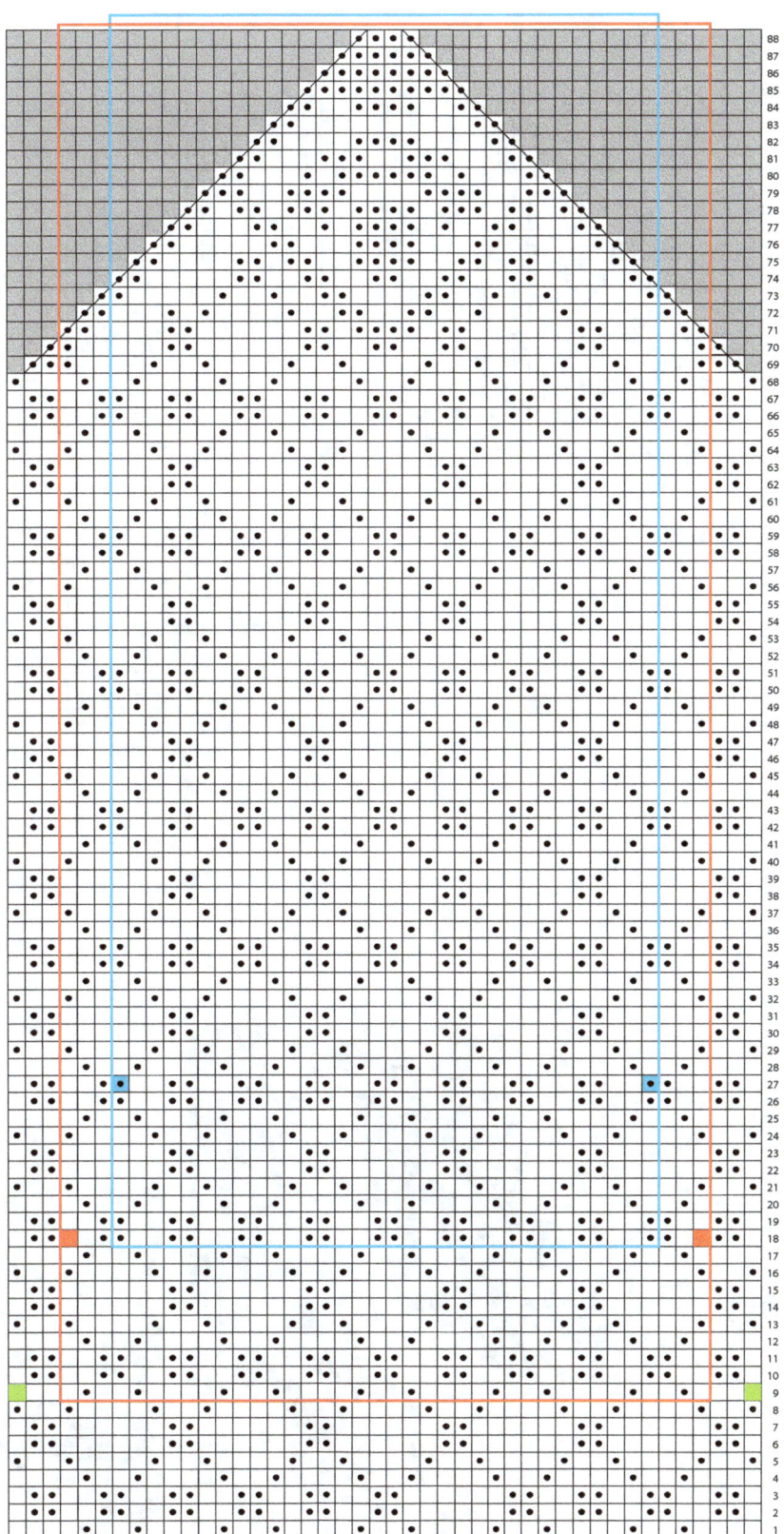

CHART B

Aurora Borealis Mittens | 86

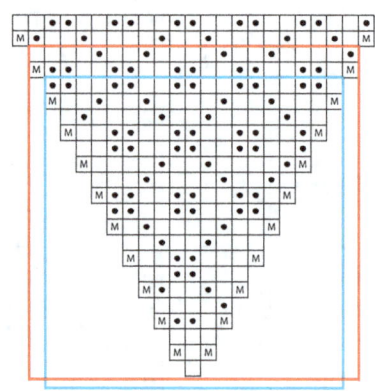

Thumb

NOTE WHAT HAPPENS WHEN YOU SWITCH THE COLORS USED FOR MC AND CC

Dagmar

BECAUSE I AM A HISTORY NERD, I HAVE ODD BRAIN-LINKS between unrelated things. Dagmar, queen consort of Denmark in the early 1200s, begged her husband from her deathbed not to marry the "beautiful flower" Berengaria from Portugal after she was gone. (*Which, of course, he went out and did anyway*). On one side of the mittens: flowers reaching for the sky; on the other, a restrictive gate. And you wonder why Aud & co ran off to Iceland for considerably more freedom?

Sizes

Women's M (L)

Blue and white pair shown in Large, with Cuff Option 7

Blue and grey pair shown in Large, with Cuff Option 7

Finished Measurements

10.5 (12)" / 26.67 (30.48)cm circumference

8.6 (10)" / 21.84 (25.4)cm high without cuff

Materials

Anzula Squishy [80% superwash merino wool, 10% nylon, 10% cashmere; 385 yds / 352m per 115g skein]; color Cornflower, and Baah! Yarns La Jolla [100% superwash merino wool; 400 yds / 365m per 100g skein]; color La Perla

Knit Picks Palette yarn [100% Peruvian highland wool; 231 yds / 211m per 50g skein]; colors: Asphalt Heather and Opal Heather.

1 set US #1/2.25 mm needles, or size needed to obtain gauge. Choose needles for knitting in the round over a small circumference: dpns, two circulars, or one long circular for magic loop, as you prefer.

Waste yarn or stitch holder for thumb stitches

Stitch markers

Large-eyed, blunt sewing needle

Gauge

32 sts x 36 rnds = 4"/10cm square in stitch pattern.

Notes

Work the stitches inside the red rectangle for medium size.

If you are working the largest size, work all the stitches.

The red solid square is for medium thumb gusset placement.

The green solid square is for large thumb gusset placement.

Hands, however, are as unique as you are. Try on your mitten, you may need to move the gusset start up or down a few rounds.

Pattern

Cuff

Cast on 84 (96) sts. Being careful not to twist, join to work in the round.

Work the cuff of your choice, as described on page 11.

Hand

Using chart A for the back of hand, and Chart B for the palm, work as follows:

Medium: Work the stitches within both red rectangles.

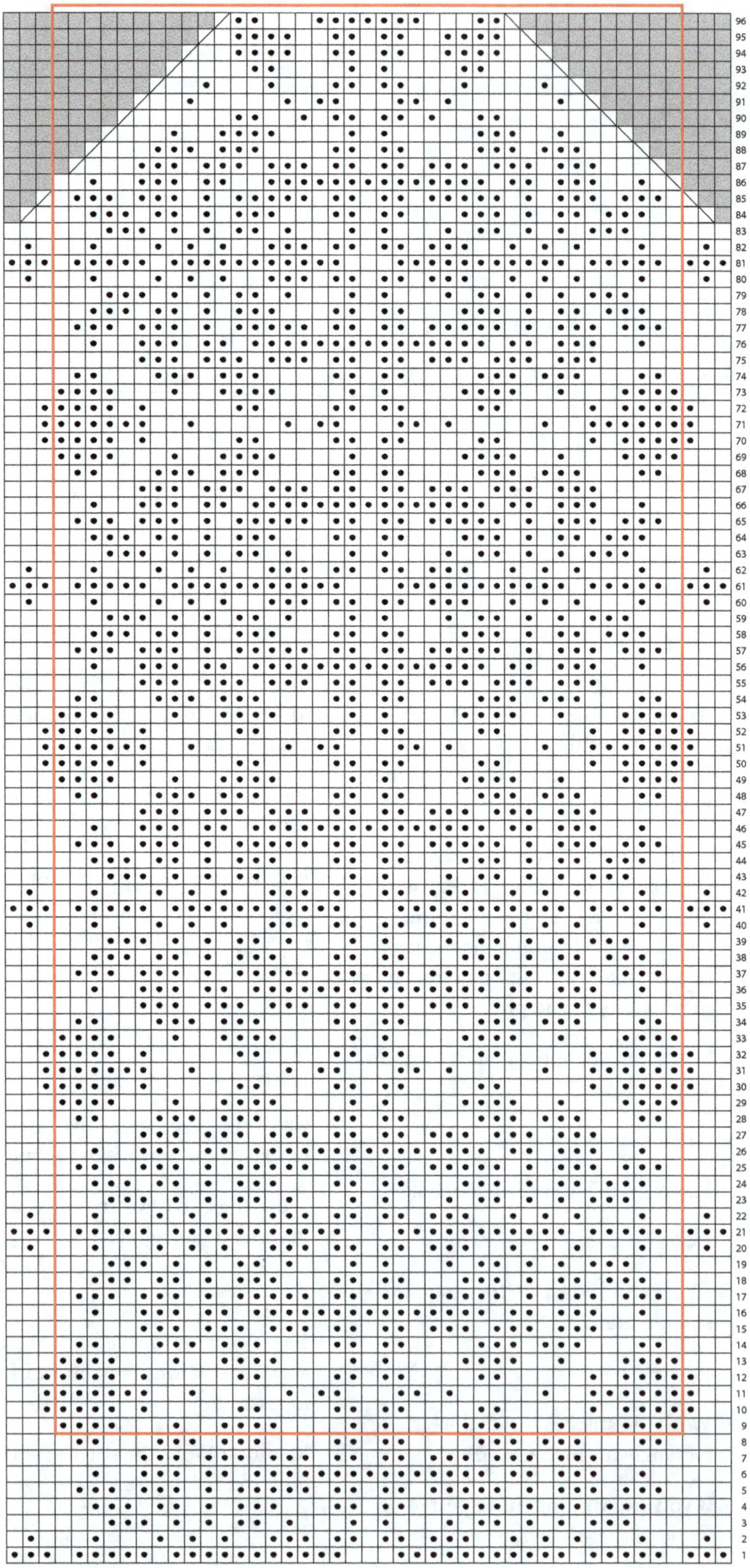

Aurora Borealis Mittens | 90

Chart A

Large: Work the whole chart. Work as set, until rnd 18 (9).

Thumb Gusset

All sizes

Left hand: Place a stitch marker either side of the color coded stitch for your size on the right hand side of your rectangle. Work the gusset chart between the stitch markers.

Right hand: Place a stitch marker either side of the color coded square for your size on the left hand side of your rectangle. Work the gusset chart between the stitch markers.

Work the hand charts as set until all increases have been completed.

Try on your mitten. Gusset length is as individual as you are. You may want to add some extra rounds before separating the thumb sts, you may also want to add some extra increases. It all depends on your hands. If you are adding extra rounds, just continue your thumb stitch pattern as set.

Once your thumb gusset is the length you want it, divide for the thumb as follows:

Work in pattern to first stitch marker, place the thumb sts on waste yarn or a stitch holder, cast on one st, work to the end of the round.

Continue to work the hand charts, as set until the last round is completed.

Break CC, and with MC, kitchener stitch the hand closed.

Thumb

Place your thumb sts back onto your needles, cast on 3 sts. - 24 (26) sts.

Work the appropriate thumb chart. Break CC, with MC, kitchener stitch the thumb closed. Work the appropriate thumb chart. Break CC, with MC, kitchener stitch the thumb closed.

Stranded colorwork thumbs tend to be narrower than you'd expect. Try working your thumb with MC only, and use a duplicate stitch in CC for your stitch pattern after the thumb is completed.

Finishing

Weave in all ends, and wet block.

Picot edgings are always beautiful but somehow, on Dagmar, it emphasizes the floral pattern even more and reminds me of Delft tile, Chinese blue willow crockery, and more...

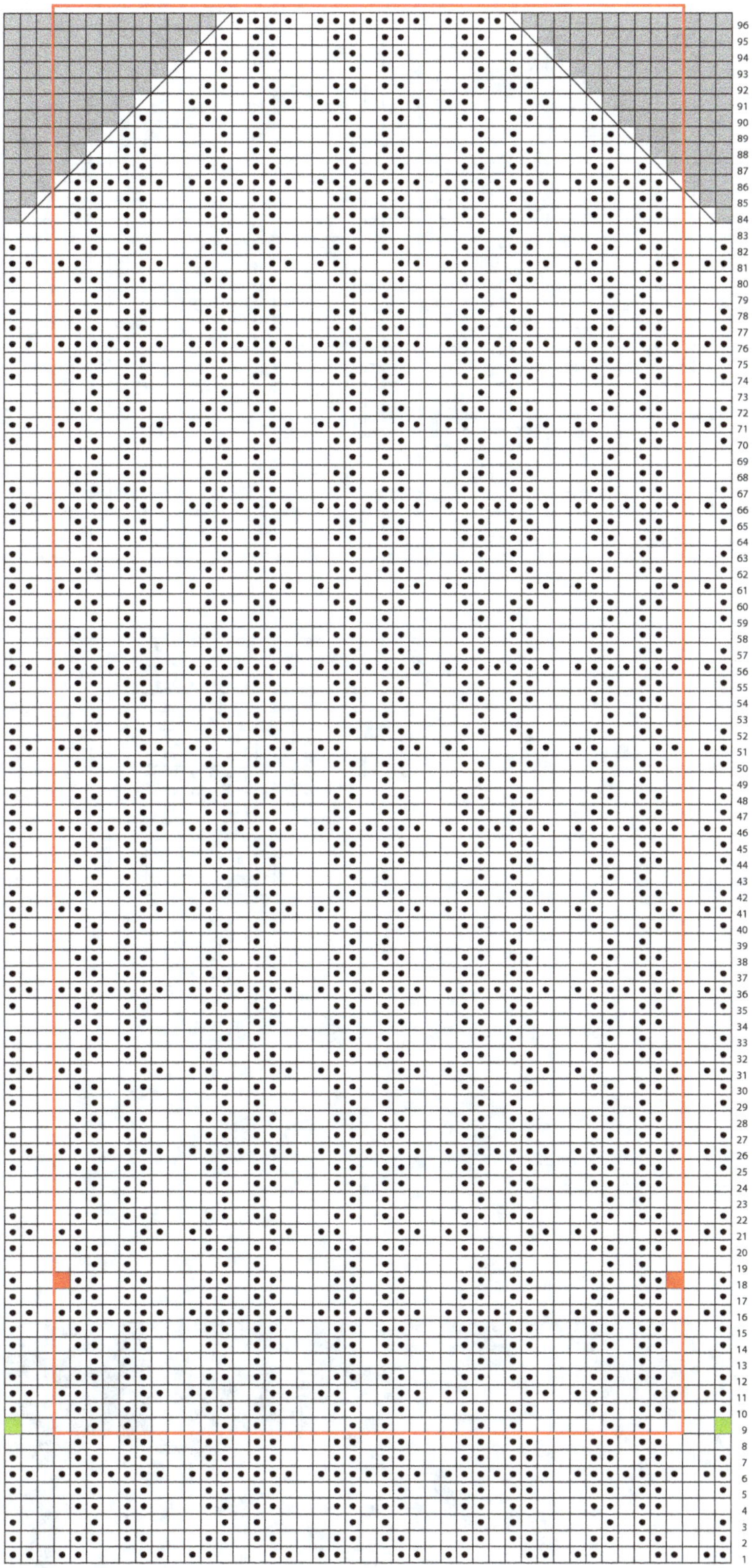

CHART B

Aurora Borealis Mittens | 92

Thumb

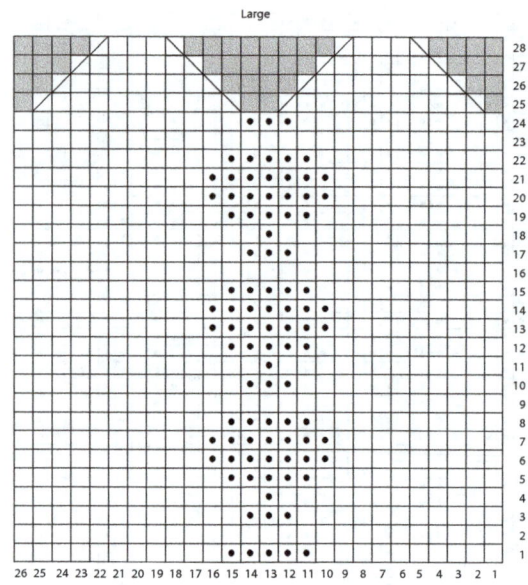

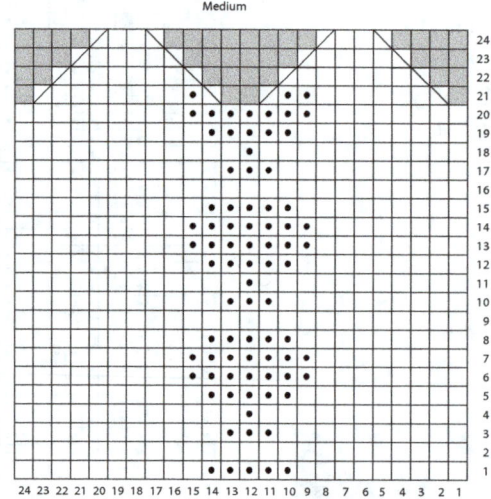

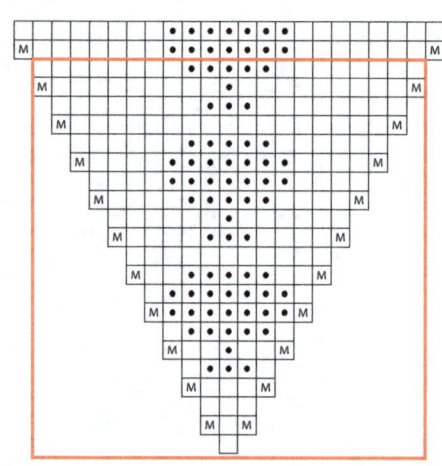

A pansy-like repetitive pattern named after a nineteenth-century Swedish diminutive of the names Gunilla or Gunhildr that implies sweetness or cuteness. *Gull* is also the Old Norse word for 'gold,' and if you've ready almost any northern fairytales, you know there's always lots of gold!

Sizes

Women's M, L

Shown in Large, with Cuff Option 3

Finished Measurements

10.5 (12)" / 26.67 (30.48)cm circumference

8.6 (10)" / 21.84 (25.4)cm high without cuff

Materials

Fable Fibers Folktale yarn [100% superwash merino wool; 400 yds / 366m per 100g skein]; colors: Chloe and Stardust

1 set US #1/2.25 mm needles, or size needed to obtain gauge. Choose needles for knitting in the round over a small circumference: dpns, two circulars, or one long circular for magic loop, as you prefer.

Waste yarn or stitch holder for thumb stitches

Stitch markers

Large-eyed, blunt sewing needle

Gauge

32 sts x 36 rnds = 4"/10cm square in stitch pattern.

Notes

Work the stitches inside the red rectangle for medium size.

If you are working the largest size, work all the stitches.

The red solid square is for medium thumb gusset placement.

The green solid square is for large thumb gusset placement.

Hands, however, are as unique as you are. Try on your mitten, you may need to move the gusset start up or down a few rounds.

Pattern

Cuff

Cast on 84 (96) sts. Being careful not to twist, join to work in the round.

Work the cuff of your choice, as described on page 11.

Hand

Using chart A for the back of hand, and Chart B for the palm, work as follows:

Medium: Work the stitches within both red rectangles.

Large: Work the whole chart.

Work as set, until rnd 18 (9).

Thumb Gusset

All sizes

Left hand: Place a stitch marker either side of the color coded stitch for your size on the right hand side of

Aurora Borealis Mittens | 96

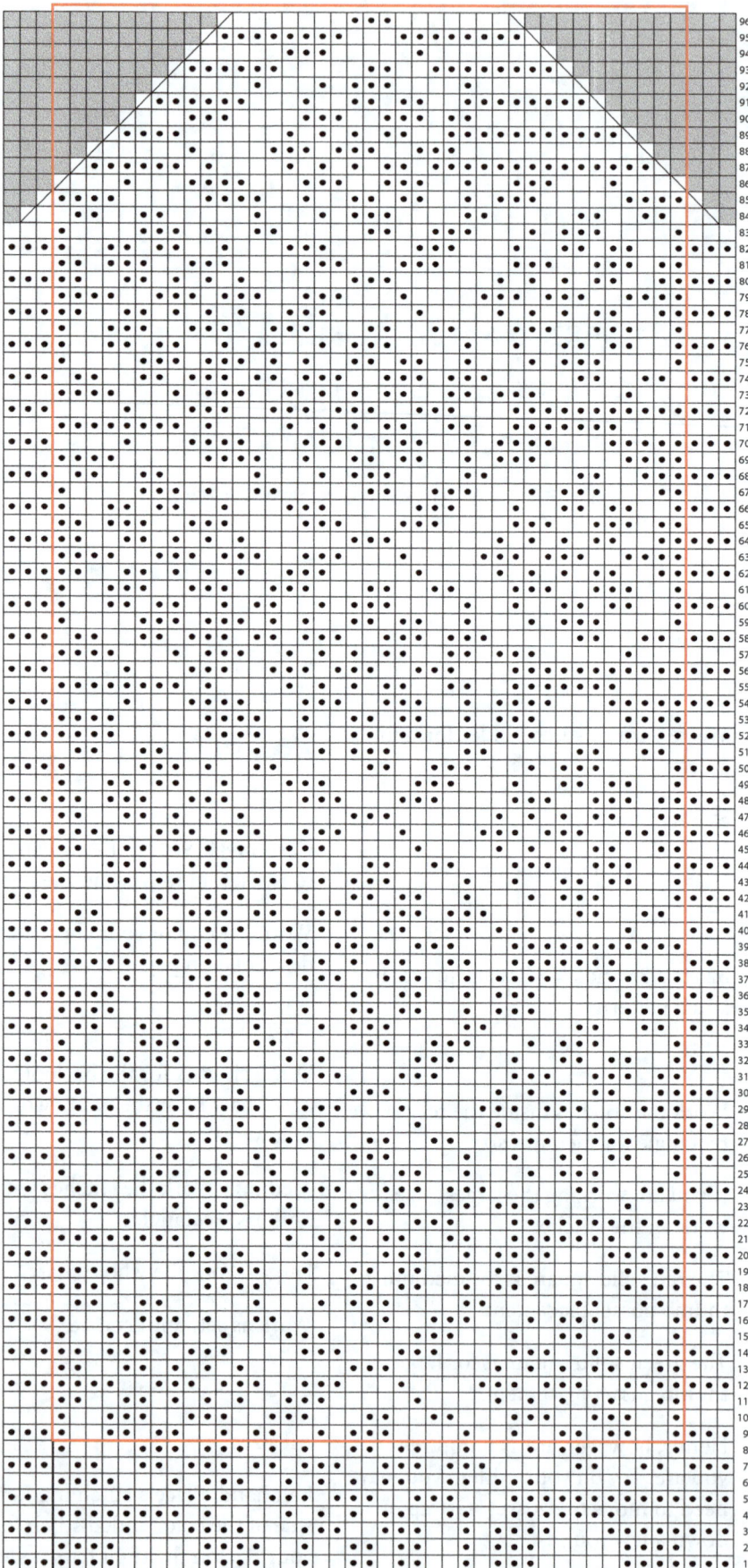

CHART A

your rectangle. Work the gusset chart between the stitch markers.

Right hand: Place a stitch marker either side of the color coded square for your size on the left hand side of your rectangle. Work the gusset chart between the stitch markers.

Work the hand charts as set until all increases have been completed.

Try on your mitten. Gusset length is as individual as you are. You may want to add some extra rounds before separating the thumb sts, you may also want to add some extra increases. It all depends on your hands. If you are adding extra rounds, just continue your thumb stitch pattern as set.

Once your thumb gusset is the length you want it, divide for the thumb as follows:

Work in pattern to first stitch marker, place the thumb sts on waste yarn or a stitch holder, cast on one st, work to the end of the round.

Continue to work the hand charts, as set until the last round is completed.

Break CC, and with MC, kitchener stitch the hand closed.

Thumb

Place your thumb sts back onto your needles, cast on 3 sts. - 24 (26) sts.

Work the appropriate thumb chart. Break CC, with MC, kitchener stitch the thumb closed.

Stranded colorwork thumbs tend to be narrower than you'd expect. Try working your thumb with MC only, and use a duplicate stitch in CC for your stitch pattern after the thumb is completed.

Finishing

Weave in all ends, and wet block.

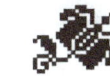

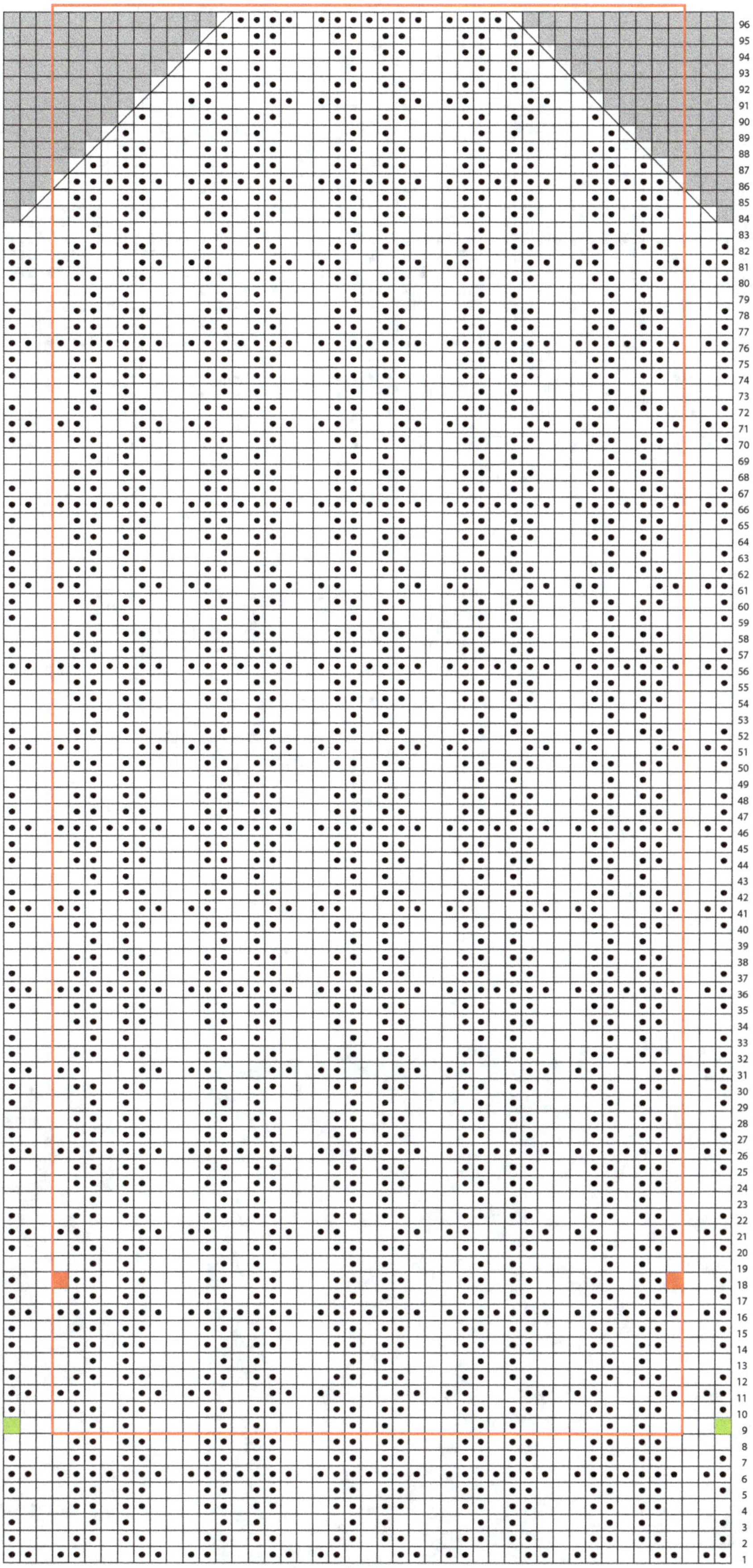
96
95
94
93
92
91
90
89
88
87
86
85
84
83
82
81
80
79
78
77
76
75
74
73
72
71
70
69
68
67
66
65
64
63
62
61
60
59
58
57
56
55
54
53
52
51
50
49
48
47
46
45
44
43
42
41
40
39
38
37
36
35
34
33
32
31
30
29
28
27
26
25
24
23
22
21
20
19
18
17
16
15
14
13
12
11
10
9
8
7
6
5
4
3
2
1

Chart B

Aurora Borealis Mittens | 98

Large

Thumb

Medium

Nordic Stars Tam

Sample knitter Kim Craigs couldn't help herself. She wanted to take one of the mitten pattern motifs and extend it into a hat. How could I say anything but "go for it?" This is the result. Though she knit it from stash, with most yarns' total yardage in this book, you should easily be able to knit both a pair of mittens and a matching hat.

Sizes

One, to fit average adult head.

(*Take note: I've got a fairly massive skull and it fits me just fine! The tam definitely stretches unless you are a very tight knitter. Again, be cautious about your gauge*).

Finished Measurements

10.5 (12)" / 26.67 (30.48)cm circumference

8.6 (10)" / 21.84 (25.4)cm high without cuff

Materials

Araucania Ranco Solid: [75% Wool/25% Nylon; 376 yds / 344m per 100g skein]; colors: 119 and 491

1 set US #0/2 mm DPNs, or size needed to obtain gauge.

US#2 / 2.75mm 16" / 40cm circular needle.

US#2 / 2.75 dpns (for crown)

Stitch markers

Large-eyed, blunt sewing needle

Gauge

35 sts x 40 rnds = 4"/10cm square in stranded stitch pattern on US#2 / 2.75mm.

Notes

Stitches Used

Double Decrease - Slip 2 sts knitwise, k1, p2sso.

M1 - make 1 by lifting the bar between the next two sts, knit into the bar.

Pattern

With US# 0 / 2mm and Color 1, cast on 144 stitches. Join to work in the round, being careful not to twist.

Rnd 1: [K2, p2], repeat to end of rnd.

Rnds 2 and 3: As rnd 1.

Rnd 4: As rnd 1, with Color 2.

Rnds 5 - 9: As rnd 1 with Color 1.

Switch to larger needles.

Increase rnd: [K3, m1]; repeat to end of rnd. 192 sts.

Next rnd: Knit in Color 1.

Using both colors, work Chart A. The chart will be worked 8 times in each rnd.

After completing the Chart A, continue with Chart B.

Break yarns, and thread through remaining stitches, and pull tight.

Weave in all ends. Wash or dampen the tam and stretch it over a dinner plate to dry.

Aurora Borealis Mittens | 102

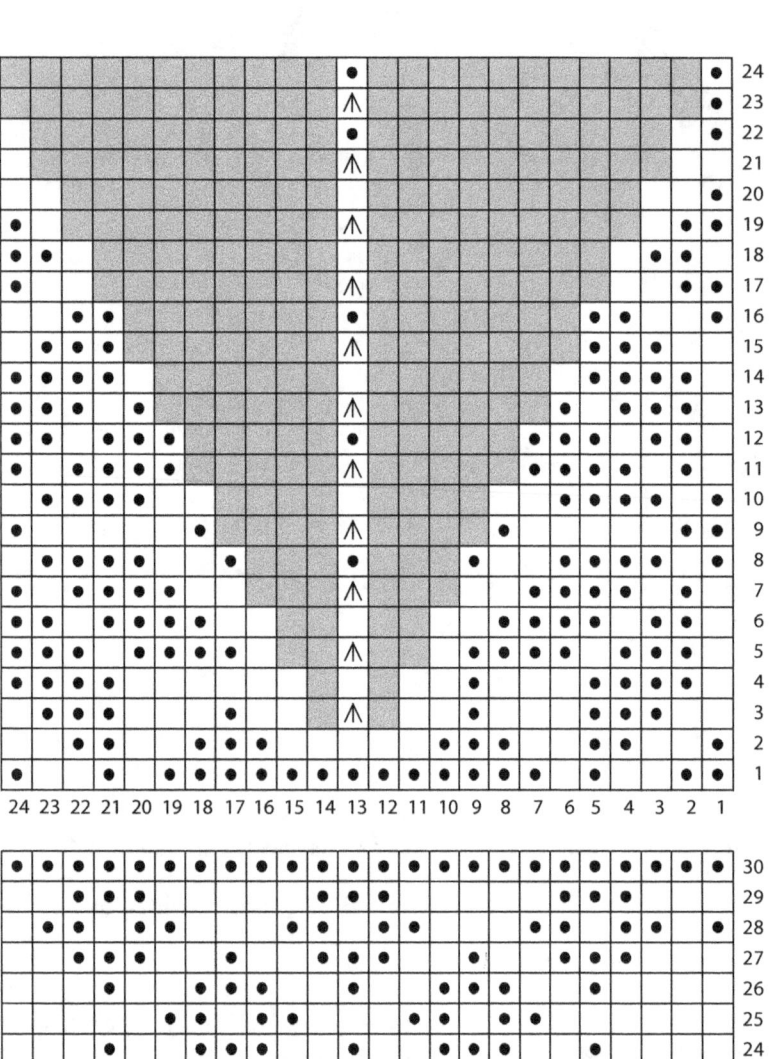

Nordic Stars Tam | 103

	No Stitch
	MC - Main Color
●	CC - Contrast Color
⋀	Double Decrease - Slip 2 sts knitwise, k1, p2sso

Epic Knitters: the saga

LIKE A VIKING RAID, IT TAKES A BOATLOAD OF PEOPLE TO attack a project this big. The knitters who helped bring this book to life are listed below. So many of them are talented designers and writers in their own right that it was a real honor to have them involved with the book. Follow our group Pinterest board at https://www.pinterest.com/knitgrrl/aurora-borealis-mittens/

Shannon Okey

pattern designer, knitter cheerleader, part-Viking

Shannon has been a full-time knit designer, author and publisher for the past decade. She has been obsessed with various knitterly northern islands since the age of seven, when she wrote a terrible poem about the Hebrides that won a writing contest. Shannon comes from the land of the ice and snow, i.e. Cleveland, Ohio, where she lives with her husband and four cats. She is knitgrrl just about everywhere, including Twitter, Ravelry and Pinterest, as well as knitgrrl.com

Andi Smith

tech editor and Shannon's favorite shield maiden

Shannon may have designed the patterns in this book but Andi brought them to *life*. Andi has been knitting for over forty years, which is why she's so good at taking things out of Shannon's notes and making sure they actually work. She served as shieldmaiden more than once during the creation of this book, making sure that the knitters' questions were fielded while Shannon was traveling. Andi is the author of *Big Foot Knits* (also from Cooperative Press) and can be found online at knitbrit.com. You want her on your shield wall, you really do.

Adrienne Martini
Angela Myers
Anna-Liza Armfield
Anne Hamilton Bean
Bex Oliger
Candace Musmeci
Cheryl Clemons
Christina Bowers
Deborah Cote-Closter
Denise Layman
Francesca Hoffman
Heather Ordover
Heather Vance
Jacquie Chalmers
Julia Stone
Kai Rochford
Karma Kauffman
Kim Craigs
Laura Hall Briedis
Linda Rockwell
Malia Arguello
Marie Duquette
Marta Poling
Penny Shima Glanz
Rebecca Conner
Rebecca Oerkfitz Garcia
Shannon Russell
Tanis Gray

Heroic Dyers

WITHOUT KNITTERS THERE WOULD BE NO KNITS, TRUE, BUT what about the dyers and yarn producers who bring us the lovely skeins we treasure? These dyers are responsible for a sizeable quantity of my own personal yarn-hoard; you should definitely check them out when adding to your stash. These are some of the yarns used during the production of this book.

Baah Yarn
Blue Moon Fiber Arts
Cascade Yarns
Cephalopod Yarns
Dragonfly Fibers
Fable Fibers
Fiber Optic
Freia Handpaints
KFI
Knit Picks
Malabrigo
Neighborhood Fiber Co
Quince & Co
The Unique Sheep

Sources for the curious

ONCE A HISTORY GRAD STUDENT, ALWAYS A HISTORY GRAD student. I love stories and folktales, but I also approach them with a critical mind. If you want to dive deeper into some of the stories and personalities behind the names of these mittens, here are some links for you.

General sources

Norse-Mythology.org is a smart and well-organized site with a lot of links to additional books you may enjoy (its creator Dan McCoy is the author of *The Love of Destiny: The Sacred and the Profane in Germanic Polytheism*, a title only a former history grad student like me could love, because Germanic polytheism is actually what I was writing about while I was still pursuing that degree).

On the general topic of fairy tales and the history and sociology behind them, see *From the Beast to the Blonde: On Fairy Tales and Their Tellers* by Marina Warner, a favorite book of mine.

Women's Work: The First 20,000 Years by Elizabeth Wayland Barber is a longtime favorite of mine because it shows the intimate connection between women's history and cloth production.

Viking Clothing by Thor Ewing really delves deep into the archaeological finds behind Viking textiles and shows how they really evolved into a fashion-loving people through textile trade and production, it's the sort of historical book you will love if you're a textile person.

Woven into the Earth: Textile Finds in Norse Greenland by Else Østergård is another favorite of mine.

Ragnar Loðbrók and Thora

Ragnar and Thora's story is included in *Ragnarssona þáttr*, The Tale of Ragnar's Sons, ably retold in this Wikipedia article. You can also read it in facing Norse and English text at this website. Ragnar is the main character of the History Channel series Vikings, which is honestly one of the better on-screen depictions of this era I've seen, and several of the characters after whom these mittens are named make appearances.

Ragnar Loðbrók and Aslaug

Ragnars saga Loðbrókar, The Tale of Ragnar Loðbrók, is part of the Völsunga saga, and tells Aslaug's origin story. Ragnar marries her after the death of Thora. She also appears in Snorri Sturluson's Edda. I have my doubts about some of the stories about Aslaug, since they are almost perfect reproductions of some classic fairy tale or folk story archetypes, but they're fun to read anyway, as all good stories are. Check out Aslaug's Wikipedia entry for the basics and additional links.

Aud the Deep-Minded

Aud the Deep-Minded, aka *Auðr djúpúðga Ketilsdóttir* is referenced in many, many sagas and early Icelandic texts due to her position as one of the earliest settlers in Iceland, including *Landnámabók*, *Njáls saga*, *Laxdæla saga*, *Eyrbyggja saga*, *Eiríks saga rauða* and *Grettis saga*. As the daughter and granddaughter of regional military commanders, you can imagine her strength of character and what dinner table conversation must have been like at family gatherings, so it is hardly surprising that after marrying and bearing children to Olaf the White, the self-proclaimed King of Dublin (Dublin, of course, got its start as a city that developed from a Norse trading post), she ended up secretly building an ocean-going ship, sailed to Orkney, where she married off one of her granddaughters, then headed for Iceland. She successfully commanded a ship full of male settlers, and was greatly respected.

Gudrid the Far Traveler

So many Gudrids and Snorris, it can be hard to keep them all apart! Halldora, whose mittens appear on page XX, had a mother in law named Gudrid, but the Gudrid I really like to read about is known as Gudrid Vidforla, "The Far-Traveler" who appears in the Vinland sagas. You can read more about her in Nancy Marie Brown's *The Far Traveler: Voyages of a Viking Woman*. She not only makes it all the way to North America, to the Vinland settlement, but also to Rome and elsewhere. (If you prefer fiction to non-, she is featured in Margaret Elphinstone's novel *The Sea Road* as well). What she thought of Freydis, another Vinland-traveler, no one knows...

Larissa Brown, author of *Beautiful Wreck*, another Cooperative Press book with plenty of Vikings also recommends *Gods' Daughter* by Heather Day Gilbert on the subject of Gudrid.